0891079661

A HUNGER
FOR GOD

Love Your Enemies:
Jesus' Love Command in the Synoptic Gospels
and the Early Christian Paraenesis

The Justification of God:
An Exegetical and Theological Study of Romans 9:1-23

Desiring God:
Meditations of a Christian Hedonist

The Supremacy of God
in Preaching

The Pleasures of God:
Meditations on God's Delight in Being God

Recovering Biblical Manhood and Womanhood:
A Response to Evangelical Feminism
(edited with Wayne Grudem)

Let the Nations Be Glad:
The Supremacy of God in Missions

Future Grace

A HUNGER FOR GOD

*Desiring God
Through Fasting and Prayer*

JOHN PIPER

CROSSWAY BOOKS • WHEATON, ILLINOIS
A DIVISION OF GOOD NEWS PUBLISHERS

A Hunger for God

Copyright © 1997 by John Piper

Published by Crossway Books
        a division of Good News Publishers
        1300 Crescent Street
        Wheaton, Illinois 60187

Cover photo: Tony Stone Images / Brett Baunton

Cover design: D² DesignWorks

ISBN: 0-7394-1136-5

Printed in the United States of America

Unless otherwise indicated, Bible quotations are taken from *The New American Standard Bible*, copyright © 1960, 1962, 1963, 1968, 1971, 1972, 1975, and 1977 by The Lockman Foundation, and are used by permission.

To my fellow elders
of Bethlehem Baptist Church,
who hunger with me
for the fullness of God,
and feast with me
at the table of grace.

CONTENTS

PREFACE

Beware of books on fasting. The Bible is very careful to warn us about people who "advocate abstaining from foods, which God created to be gratefully shared in by those who believe and know the truth" (1 Timothy 4:1-3). The apostle Paul asks with dismay, "Why . . . do you submit yourself to decrees, such as 'Do not handle, do not taste, do not touch'?" (Colossians 2:20-21). He is jealous for the full enjoyment of Christian liberty. Like a great declaration of freedom over every book on fasting flies the banner, "Food will not commend us to God; we are neither the worse if we do not eat, nor the better if we do eat" (1 Corinthians 8:8). There once were two men. One said, "I fast twice a week"; the other said, "God be merciful to me a sinner." Only one went down to his house justified (Luke 18:12-14).

The discipline of self-denial is fraught with dangers—perhaps only surpassed by the dangers of indulgence. These also we are warned about: "All things are lawful for me, *but I will not be mastered by anything*" (1 Corinthians 6:12). What masters us has become our god; and Paul warns us about those "whose god is their appetite" (Philippians 3:19). Appetite dictates the direction of their lives. The stomach is sovereign. This has a religious expression and an irreligious one. Religiously "persons . . . turn the grace of our God into licentiousness" (Jude 4) and tout the slogan, "Food is for the stomach and the stomach is for food" (1 Corinthians 6:13). Irreligiously, with no pretext of pardoning grace, persons simply yield to "the desires for other things [that] enter in and choke the word" (Mark 4:19).

"Desires for other things"—there's the enemy. And the only weapon that will triumph is a deeper hunger for God. The weakness of our hunger for God is not because he is unsavory, but because we keep ourselves stuffed with "other things." Perhaps, then, the denial of our stomach's appetite for food might express, or even increase, our soul's appetite for God.

What is at stake here is not just the good of our souls, but also the glory of God. God is most glorified in us when we are most satisfied in him. The fight of faith is a fight to feast on all that God is for us in Christ. What we hunger for most, we worship.

> *His goodness shines with brightest rays*
> *When we delight in all his ways.*
> *His glory overflows its rim*
> *When we are satisfied in him.*
> *His radiance will fill the earth*
> *When people revel in his worth.*
> *The beauty of God's holy fire*
> *Burns brightest in the heart's desire.*

Between the dangers of self-denial and self-indulgence there is a path of pleasant pain. It is not the pathological pleasure of a masochist, but the passion of a lover's quest: "I have suffered the loss of all things, and count them but rubbish in order that I may gain Christ" (Philippians 3:8). That is the path we will try to follow in this book.

That I could even attempt the journey is owing to God's grace, which I live on every day. It has come to me in Jesus who loved me and gave himself for me. It has come to me in my wife, Noël, who supports me in the work of preaching and writing and tending the flock. I love you, Noël, and thank you for your partnership in the great work. God has been good to us. Grace has come to me again in the faithful labors of Carol Steinbach, whose careful reading has left its mark, and whose industry created the indexes. And grace has come to me through my fellow elders at Bethlehem Baptist Church. They forged a mission statement for our church that I embrace as the mission of my life. And they gave me the charge and the time to write this book and make it a part of that mission: "We exist to spread a passion for the supremacy of God in all things for the joy of all peoples." That is my prayer for this book. When God is the supreme hunger of our hearts, he will be supreme in everything.

John Piper
May 1, 1997

Whom have I in heaven but thee?
And there is nothing upon earth
that I desire besides thee.
My flesh and my heart may fail,
but God is the strength of my heart
and my portion for ever.

—PSALM 73:25-26, RSV

Almost everywhere at all times fasting has held a place of great importance since it is closely linked with the intimate sense of religion. Perhaps this is the explanation for the demise of fasting in our day. When the sense of God diminishes, fasting disappears.

—EDWARD FARRELL[1]

INTRODUCTION

A Homesickness
for God

The birthplace of Christian fasting is homesickness for God. In the summer of 1967 I had been in love with Noël for a whole year. If you had told me then that we would have to wait another year and a half to marry, I would have protested firmly. For us, it seemed, the sooner the better. It was the summer before my senior year in college. I was working as a water safety instructor at a Christian athletic camp in South Carolina. She was hundreds of miles away working as a waitress.

Never had I known an aching like this one. I had been homesick before, but never like this. Every day I would write her a letter and talk about this longing. In the late morning, just before lunch, there would be mail call. When I heard my name and saw the lavender envelope, my appetite would be taken away. Or, more accurately, my hunger for food was silenced by the hunger of my heart. Often, instead of eating lunch with the campers, I would take the letter to a quiet place in the woods and sit down on the leaves for a different kind of meal. It wasn't the real thing. But the color, the smell, the script, the message, the signature were foretastes. And with them, week by week, I was strengthened in hope, and the reality just over the horizon was kept alive in my heart.

The Romance and the Resistance of Fasting

Christian fasting, at its root, is the hunger of a homesickness for God. But the story of my heart-hunger to be with Noël could be misleading. It tells only half the story of Christian fasting. Half of Christian fasting is that our physical appetite is lost because our homesickness for God is so intense. The other half is that our homesickness for God is threatened because our physical appetites are so intense. In the first half, appetite is lost. In the second half, appetite is resisted. In the first, we yield to the higher hunger that is. In the second, we fight for the higher hunger that isn't. Christian fasting is not only the spontaneous effect of a superior satisfaction in God; it is also a chosen weapon against every force in the world that would take that satisfaction away.

God's Greatest Adversaries Are His Gifts

The greatest enemy of hunger for God is not poison but apple pie. It is not the banquet of the wicked that dulls our appetite for heaven, but endless nibbling at the table of the world. It is not the X-rated video, but the prime-time dribble of triviality we drink in every night. For all the ill that Satan can do, when God describes what keeps us from the banquet table of his love, it is a piece of land, a yoke of oxen, and a wife (Luke 14:18-20). The greatest adversary of love to God is not his enemies but his gifts. And the most deadly appetites are not for the poison of evil, but for the simple pleasures of earth. For when these replace an appetite for God himself, the idolatry is scarcely recognizable, and almost incurable.

Jesus said some people hear the word of God, and a desire

for God is awakened in their hearts. But then, "as they go on their way they are choked with worries and riches and *pleasures of this life*" (Luke 8:14). In another place he said, "*The desires for other things* enter in and choke the word, and it becomes unfruitful" (Mark 4:19). "The pleasures of this life" and "the desires for other things"—these are not evil in themselves. These are not vices. These are gifts of God. They are your basic meat and potatoes and coffee and gardening and reading and decorating and traveling and investing and TV-watching and Internet-surfing and shopping and exercising and collecting and talking. And all of them can become deadly substitutes for God.

The Deadening Effects of Innocent Delights

Therefore, when I say that the root of Christian fasting is the hunger of homesickness for God, I mean that we will do anything and go without anything if, by any means, we might protect ourselves from the deadening effects of innocent delights and preserve the sweet longings of our homesickness for God. Not just food, but anything. Several years ago I called our people to fast for a twenty-four-hour period once a week (breakfast and lunch on Wednesdays, if possible) during the month of January. We were facing huge issues of self-assessment and direction, and we needed the fullness of God's presence with all his wisdom and purifying power. Within a few days I got this note in the mail:

> I'm behind this. I think God is in it. It doesn't work for me on Wednesday. I'm with people over lunch every day. So I have a couple of things I believe are from the Spirit that may be more of a fast for some than food. I thought not watching television for a week, or for a month, or a night of the week when I normally watch it, might be more of a fast than food. Instead of watching my favorite program, I might

spend the time talking and listening to God. I wonder if there might be others for whom this would be a fast and would be a focused time of prayer to them.

I said to the congregation the next Sunday, "Amen. If you say, 'Fasting on Wednesday doesn't work for me,' that's okay. If your heart is right and you're open to the Lord and you're asking him, 'Lord, draw me into the spirit of awakening through fasting,' he will show you. He'll show you when and how. If your health doesn't allow for that, if the doctor says, 'No fasting for you,' that's fine. The Great Physician knows all about that, and something else will work for you."

The issue is not food *per se*. The issue is anything and everything that is, or can be, a substitute for God. Martyn Lloyd-Jones (1899-1981), the pastor of Westminster Chapel in London, delivered a great sermon on fasting when he was preaching through the Sermon on the Mount in 1959-1960. In it he said,

> Fasting if we conceive of it truly, must not . . . be confined to the question of food and drink; fasting should really be made to include abstinence from anything which is legitimate in and of itself for the sake of some special spiritual purpose. There are many bodily functions which are right and normal and perfectly legitimate, but which for special peculiar reasons in certain circumstances should be controlled. That is fasting.[2]

My assumption so far has been that good things can do great damage. Oxen and fields and marriage can keep you out of the kingdom of heaven. Which is why Jesus says, "No one of you can be my disciple who does not bid farewell to *all his own possessions*" (Luke 14:33, author's translation[3]). *Anything* can stand in the way of true discipleship—not just evil, and not just food, but anything. Nor should it be surprising that the greatest competitors for our devotion and affection for God would be some of his most precious gifts.

When Abraham Preferred God to the Life of His Son

How does fasting help us keep from turning gifts into gods? Consider the almost-sacrifice of Isaac by his father Abraham. When Abraham had stretched out his hand to kill his son and the heir of God's promise, "the angel of the LORD called to him from heaven, and said, 'Abraham, Abraham!' And he said, 'Here I am.' And he said, 'Do not stretch out your hand against the lad, and do nothing to him; for now I know that you fear God, since you have not withheld your son, your only son, from Me'" (Genesis 22:11-12). Now here was a radical kind of fast: the sacrifice of a son. God did not call for this "fast" because Isaac was evil. On the contrary, it was because in Abraham's eyes he was so good. Indeed he seemed indispensable for the fulfillment of God's promise. Fasting is not the forfeit of evil but of good.

But why would God call for such a thing? Because it was a test. Does Abraham delight in the fear of the Lord (Isaiah 11:3) more than he delights in his own son? God spoke through the angel: "Now I know that you fear God, since you have not withheld your son, your only son, from Me." These words, "now I know"—what do they mean? Did God not know that Abraham was a God-fearing man and that he valued God above his son? The Bible teaches that God "knows the hearts of all men" (1 Kings 8:39; Acts 1:24); indeed, he "fashions the hearts of them all" (Psalm 33:15). Why then the test? Here is the way C. S. Lewis answers the question,

> [I am concerned with the question] "If God is omniscient he must have known what Abraham would do, without any experiment; why, then, this needless torture?" But as St.

Augustine points out, whatever God knew, Abraham at any rate did not know that this obedience would endure such a command until the event taught him; and the obedience which he did not know that he would choose, he cannot be said to have chosen. The reality of Abraham's obedience was the act itself; and what God knew in knowing that Abraham "would obey" was Abraham's actual obedience on that mountain top at that moment. To say that God "need not have tried the experiment" is to say that because God knows, the thing known by God need not exist.[4]

God wills to know the actual, lived-out reality of our preference for him over all things. And he wills that we have the testimony of our own authenticity through acts of actual preference of God over his gifts. Lewis is right that God may as well not have created the world, but only imagined it, if his knowing what "would be" is as good as his knowing it in the very act. God wills that he have an experiential-knowing, an actual seeing-knowing, a watching-knowing. A real lived-out human act of preference for God over his gifts is the actual lived-out glorification of God's excellence for which he created the world. Fasting is not the only way, or the main way, that we glorify God in preferring him above his gifts. But it is one way. And it is a way that can serve all the others.

Eating as the Anesthesia of Sadness

Lewis referred to St. Augustine. What Augustine said was this: "For the most part, the human mind cannot attain to self-knowledge otherwise than by making trial of its powers through temptation, by some kind of experimental and not merely verbal self-interrogation."[5] In other words, we easily deceive ourselves that we love God unless our love is frequently put to the test, and we must show our preferences not merely with words but with sacrifice. Admittedly the sacrifice of a son says more than the sacrifice of a sandwich. But the principle is the same. And many small acts of preferring fellowship with God above food can form a habit of communion and contentment that makes one ready for the ultimate sacrifice. This is one way that fasting serves all our acts of love to God. It keeps the preferring faculty on alert and sharp. It does not let the issue rest. It forces us to ask repeatedly: do I really hunger for God? Do I miss him? Do I long for him? Or have I begun to be content with his gifts?

Christian fasting is a test to see what desires control us. What are our bottom-line passions? In his chapter on fasting in *The Celebration of Discipline*, Richard Foster says, "More than any other discipline, fasting reveals the things that control us. This is a wonderful benefit to the true disciple who longs to be transformed into the image of Jesus Christ. We cover up what is inside of us with food and other things."[6]

Psychologically, that sort of thing is spoken of a lot today, especially in regard to people who have much pain in their lives. We would say they "medicate" their pain with food. They anesthetize themselves to the hurt inside by eating. But this is not some rare, technical syndrome. All of us do it. Everybody. No exceptions. We all ease our discomfort using food and cover our unhappiness by setting our eyes on dinnertime. Which is why fasting exposes all of us—our pain, our pride, our anger. Foster continues:

If pride controls us, it will be revealed almost immediately. David said, "I humbled my soul with fasting" [Psalm 35:13]. Anger, bitterness, jealousy, strife, fear—if they are within us, they will surface during fasting. At first, we will rationalize that our anger is due to our hunger. And then, we know that we are angry because the spirit of anger is within us. We can rejoice in this knowledge because we know that healing is available through the power of Christ.[7]

One of the reasons for fasting is to know what is in us—just as Abraham showed what was in him. In fasting it will come out. You will see it. And you will have to deal with it or quickly smother it again. When midmorning comes and you want food so badly that the thought of lunch becomes as sweet as a summer vacation, then suddenly you realize, "Oh, I forgot, I made a commitment. I can't have that pleasure. I'm fasting for lunch too." Then what are you going to do with all the unhappiness inside? Formerly, you blocked it out with the hope of a tasty lunch. The hope of food gave you the good feelings to balance out the bad feelings. But now the balance is off. You must find another way to deal with it.

The Hungry Handmaid of Faith

At these points we really begin to discover what our spiritual resources are. The things I discover about my soul are so valuable for the fight of faith. I almost subtitled this book: *Fasting—the Hungry Handmaid of Faith*. What a servant she is! Humbly and quietly, with scarcely a movement, she brings up out of the dark places of my soul the dissatisfactions in relationships, the frustrations of the ministry, the fears of failure, the emptiness of wasted time. And just when my heart begins to retreat to the delicious hope of eating supper with friends at Pizza Hut, she quietly reminds me: not tonight. It can be a devastating experience at first. Will I find spiritual communion with God sweet enough, and hope in his promises deep enough, not just to cope, but to flourish and rejoice in him? Or will I rationalize away my need to fast and retreat to the medication of food? The apostle Paul said, "I will not be mastered by anything" (1 Corinthians 6:12). Fasting reveals the measure of food's mastery over us—or television or computers or whatever we submit to again and again to conceal the weakness of our hunger for God.

Why Did God Create Bread and Hunger?

One of the reasons food has this amazing power is that it is so basic to our existence. Why is this? I mean, why did God create bread and design human beings to need it for life? He could have created life that has no need of food. He is God. He could have done it any way he pleased. Why bread? And why hunger and thirst? My answer is very simple: He created bread so that we would have some idea of what the Son of God is like when he says, "I am the bread of life" (John 6:35). And he created the rhythm of thirst and satisfaction so that we would have some idea of what faith in Christ is like when Jesus said, "He who believes in me shall never thirst" (John 6:35). God did not have to create beings who need food and water and who have capacities for pleasant tastes.

But man is not the center of the universe, God is. And everything, as Paul says, is "from him and through him and to him" (Romans 11:36). "To him" means everything exists to call attention to him and to bring admiration to him. In Colossians 1:16, Paul says more specifically that "all things were created by [Christ] and for [Christ]." Therefore bread was created for the glory of Christ. Hunger and thirst were created for the glory of Christ. And fasting was created for the glory of Christ.

Which means that bread magnifies Christ in two ways: by being eaten with gratitude for his goodness, and by being forfeited out of hunger for God himself. When we eat, we taste the emblem of our heavenly food—the Bread of Life. And when we fast we say, "I love the Reality above the emblem." In the heart of the saint both eating and fasting are worship. Both magnify Christ. Both send the heart—grateful and yearning—to the Giver. Each has its appointed place, and each has its danger. The danger of eating is that we fall in love with the gift; the danger of fasting is that we belittle the gift and glory in our willpower.

How the Book Is Organized

There is no safe and easy way home to heaven. The hard and narrow way is strewn with obstacles and many fatal paths of innocent pleasure. There is a war to be fought within and without. And one of the weapons along the way is fasting. Therefore this book has an inward and an outward thrust. It's about the inward war with our own appetites that compete with hunger for God. And it's about the outward war of revival and reformation and world evangelization and social justice and cultural engagement. Though they are deeply interwoven, the first three chapters are more inward, and the last three are more outward. And the one in the middle is a crossover chapter because longing and fasting for the coming of Christ is intensely personal but demands global engagement until he comes.

Why I Wrote This Book

My aim and my prayer in writing this book is that it might awaken a hunger for the supremacy of God in all things for the joy of all peoples. Fasting proves the presence, and fans the flame, of that hunger. It is an intensifier of spiritual desire. It is a faithful enemy of fatal bondage to innocent things. It is the physical exclamation point at the end of the sentence: "This much, O God, I long for you and for the manifestation of your glory in the world!"

One might think that those who feast most often on communion with God are least hungry. They turn often from the innocent pleasures of the world to linger more directly in the presence of God through the revelation of his Word. And there they eat the Bread of Heaven and drink the Living Water by meditation and faith. But, paradoxically, it is not so that they are the least hungry saints. The opposite is the case. The strongest, most mature Christians I have ever met are the hungriest for God. It might seem that those who eat most would be least hungry. But that's not the way it works with an inexhaustible fountain, and an infinite feast, and a glorious Lord.

When you take your stand on the finished work of God in Christ, and begin to drink at the River of Life and eat the Bread of Heaven, and know that you have found the end of all your longings, you only get hungrier for God. The more satisfaction you experience from God, while still in this world, the greater your desire for the next. For, as C. S. Lewis said, "Our best havings are wantings."[8]

The more deeply you walk with Christ, the hungrier you get *for* Christ . . . the more homesick you get for heaven . . . the more you want "all the fullness of God" . . . the more you want to be done with sin . . . the more you want the Bridegroom to come again . . . the more you want the Church revived and purified with the beauty of Jesus . . . the more you want a great awakening to God's reality in the cities . . . the more you want to see the light of the gospel of the glory of Christ penetrate the darkness of all the unreached peoples of the world . . . the more you want to see false worldviews yield to the force of Truth . . . the more you want to see pain relieved and tears wiped away and death destroyed . . . the more you long for every wrong to be made right and the justice and grace of God to fill the earth like the waters cover the sea.

If you don't feel strong desires for the manifestation of the glory of God, it is not because you have drunk deeply and are satisfied. It is because you have nibbled so long at the table of the world. Your soul is stuffed with small things, and there is no room for the great.[9] God did not create you for this. There is an appetite for God. And it can be awakened. I invite you to turn from the dulling effects of food and the dangers of idolatry, and to say with some simple fast: "This much, O God, I want you."

But the days will come
when the bridegroom
is taken away from them,
and then they will fast.

—MATTHEW 9:15

If you have died with Christ
to the elementary principles of the world,
why, as if you were living in the world,
do you submit yourself to decrees, such as,
"Do not handle, do not taste, do not touch!"
(which all refer to things destined to perish with the using)—
in accordance with the commandments
and teachings of men?
These are matters which have, to be sure,
the appearance of wisdom
in self-made religion and self-abasement
and severe treatment of the body,
but are of no value against fleshly indulgence.

—COLOSSIANS 2:20-23

I

IS FASTING CHRISTIAN?

New Fasting for the New Wine

There's a little document called the *Didache* which was written near the end of the first century. In it there is a section on fasting. One verse goes like this: "Let not your fasts be with hypocrites, for they fast on Mondays and Thursdays, but do you fast on Wednesdays and Fridays."[1] Now that seems strange. Why is changing the fast days such a big deal? I think the point of the early church was this: the Jewish custom was to celebrate its Sabbath on Saturday. That's what the Old Covenant called for. Now, to show that we have continuity and discontinuity from Judaism, we Christians will celebrate the Sabbath, but on a different day. We will celebrate on Sunday, the day the Lord rose from the dead and created a new people. In the same way the Jews did their fasting on Mondays and Thursdays, but we will do ours on different days. Why? Same reason: to show there is continuity and discontinuity. Yes, we embrace fasting; but, no, not just as we find it. There is something new about Christian fasting. We'll take it, but we'll change it. No, we don't mean that fasting on different days is what makes it Christian. That is only a pointer. But Christian fasting *is* new. That is for sure. How it is new is the point of this chapter.

In this connection, the most important word on fasting in the Bible is Matthew 9:14-17.[2] I know this is a sweeping claim for me to make. But I say it because these words of Jesus speak most directly and deeply to the central problem of fasting— namely, Is it a distinctively Christian thing to do? If so, how?

It Is Not Obvious That Fasting Is Christian

This is a crucial question for at least four reasons. First of all, fasting, as a deliberate abstinence from food for religious, cultural, political, or health reasons, is "a practice found in all societies, cultures and centuries."[3] Virtually every religion in the world practices fasting. And even non-religious people fast for political and health reasons. So why should Christians join this pagan parade of asceticism? Second, even if fasting was practiced extensively by God's people in the Old Testament, does not the arrival of the kingdom in the ministry of Jesus make this practice obsolete? Can you put the new wine of the kingdom into the old wineskins of external form and ritual? Third, does not the finished triumph of Christ on the cross, and the ongoing presence of the Holy Spirit in the church mean that the victorious Christ is so powerfully among us that the dominant spirit of life should be celebration, not mortification? And besides these three objections, does not the triumph of fasting over the body's appetites lead to pride and self-reliance, which is even worse than gluttony?

So it is not at all obvious that fasting is a distinctively Christian thing to do. If it is, we need to see how it relates to the Center. And the Center is the triumph of Christ in dying and rising and reigning over history for the salvation of his people and the glory of his Father.

Fasting Is a Universal Religious Practice

No one knows how or where fasting had its beginning.[4] Wherever you go, there are customs and traditions of fasting. Most people are aware of the Jewish fasts including Yom Kippur, or the day of Atonement (Leviticus 16:29-31),[5] and the Muslim fasting during Ramadan and the severe fasting of the Hindu high caste of Brahmans.[6] But the extent of the practice is worldwide. For example,

> the Andaman Islanders . . . abstain from certain fruits, edible roots, etc. at certain seasons, because the god Puluga . . . requires them, and would send a deluge if the taboo were broken. . . . Among the Koita of New Guinea a woman during pregnancy must not eat bandicoot, echidna, certain fish, and iguana; and the husband must observe the same food taboos. . . . Among the Yoruba, [at the death of a husband] widows and daughters are shut up and must refuse all food for at least 24 hours. . . . In British Columbia, the Stlatlumh (Lillooet) spent four days after the funeral feast in fasting, lamentations, and ceremonial ablutions. . . . Before slaying the eagle, a sacred bird, the professional eagle-killer among the Cherokees had to undergo a long vigil of prayer and fasting. . . . [Other] American Indian youth [often undergo prolonged austerities] in order that by means of a vision [they] may see the guardian spirit which will be [theirs] for the remainder of [their] life. . . . Among the tribes of New South Wales, boys at the bora ceremonies are kept for two days without food, and receive only a little water.[7]

Fasting Is a Political Weapon

In addition to worldwide religious fasting, there is also political or protest fasting. One of the most famous examples is Mahatma Gandhi, who lived from 1869 to 1948 and spent over thirty years crusading peacefully for the independence of India. His family and his Hindu culture fed his passion for fasting as a political weapon. His mother was a devout Hindu who went beyond the required duties of fasting each year and added several more rigorous fasts during the rainy season. Gandhi recalled,

> She would take the hardest vows and keep them without flinching. Living on one meal a day during the Chaturmas was a habit with her. Not content with that she fasted every alternate day during one Chaturmas. During another Chaturmas, she vowed not to have food without seeing the sun. We children on those days would stand, staring at the sky, waiting to announce the appearance of the sun to our mother. Everyone knows that at the height of the rainy season the sun does not often condescend to show his face. And I remember days when, at his sudden appearance, we would rush and announce it to her. She would run out to see with her own eyes, but by that time the fugitive sun would be gone, thus depriving her of her meal. "That does not matter," she would say cheerfully, "God did not want me to eat today." And then she would return to her round of duties.[8]

It's not surprising that Gandhi would make fasting an essential part of his political career. By the ancient laws of Manu, a creditor could only collect a debt owed him by shaming the debtor. He would sit, for example, before the debtor's house without eating day after day until the debtor was shamed into paying his debt. Eric Rogers observed that "this very Indian technique worked for Gandhi. . . . His fasting undoubtedly touched more hearts than anything else he did. Not just in India, but practically everywhere, men were haunted by the image of a frail little man cheerfully enduring privation for the sake of a principle."[9]

Fasting Is a Health Regimen

Then, besides religious and political fasting there is health fasting, with or without religious associations. A brief search on the World Wide Web under the topic "fasting" reveals hundreds of organizations and publications devoted to fasting for health. For example, one of the prominent locations is the Fasting Center International. The blurb on their Internet home page goes like this:

> Feeling out of shape, self-conscious, low on energy, or down-right unhealthy? Want to improve your physical health, while heightening your clarity of consciousness and your spirituality, as well? Scientific juice-fasting enables you to accomplish all of these goals, very quickly, without any interruption of your work, life, exercise or study routines. Fact is, you'll experience more energy than you now have, during and after your fast!

Glimpses like these, of worldwide religious, political, and health fasting, free us from the notion that fasting, in and of itself, is peculiarly Christian. It may, in fact, be emphatically anti-Christian, as it was already in the New Testament, when forty men "bound themselves under a curse not to eat or drink" until they had killed the apostle Paul (Acts 23:21). And it may be distorted, even among Christians, not only into legalistic technique (as we will see), but also into a destructive bondage like anorexia nervosa.[10] All of this raises the question why a Christian would put much stock in a ritual so widely used for non-Christian religious, political, and fitness purposes.

Does Fasting Belong in the Kingdom of God?

Not only that, the prevalence of fasting in the Old Testament raises the question whether the practice has abiding validity for people who live on this side of the coming of the Messiah and the appearance of the kingdom of God. Jesus said, "If I cast out demons by the finger of God, then *the kingdom of God has come upon you*" (Luke 11:20). And when the Pharisees asked about the coming of the kingdom, he said, "*The kingdom of God is in your midst*" (Luke 17:21). So there is a profound sense in which the long-awaited kingdom of God has *already* come in the life and ministry of Jesus.

This is the "mystery of the kingdom" that Jesus had in mind when he said to his disciples, "To you has been given the mystery of the kingdom of God; but those who are outside get everything in parables" (Mark 4:11). This was a stunning new reality in the world. "The new truth, now given to men by revelation in the person and mission of Jesus, is that *the Kingdom which is to come finally in apocalyptic power, as foreseen in Daniel, has in fact entered into the world in advance in a hidden form to work secretly within and among men.*"[11]

So the question is pressing: does fasting belong in the Church—the new kingdom-people that God is assembling from all the peoples of the world? Some think not. For example, in his book, *Prayer and Fasting: A Study in the Devotional Life of the Early Church,* Keith Main argues that the inbreaking of the kingdom of God in Jesus' ministry radically changes the importance of fasting. "Thus far," he says, "we have suggested that the joy and thanksgiving that marks the prayer life of the New Testament is a sign of the inbreaking of the Kingdom of God. *Fasting is no longer consistent with the joyous and thankful attitude that marks the fellowship.*"[12]

Does Paul Nullify Fasting?

Keith Main's viewpoint gains more credibility when we look at the rest of the New Testament outside the Gospels. Fasting is barely visible.[13] Main presses his point:

> *[Fasting] ceases to be a crucial issue within the church.* . . .
> Paul, following the lead of Jesus, deliberately diverted the
> disciples' attention away from fasting and any form of food
> asceticism and into prayer, service, and toil on behalf of the
> Kingdom. Missionary work served as a corrective and coun-
> terpoise not only to apocalyptic dreaming but also to the
> outworn and overworked custom of fasting. . . . A sense of
> Life Eternal is ever breaking in upon us. The believer
> marches to the sound of music from a different world! And
> it is exceedingly difficult to reconcile the Risen Christ with
> the fasting forms.[14]

Does the scarcity of fasting in the New Testament epistles,
and the joyful presence of the kingdom and the glorious ministry
of the Spirit of Christ nullify the relevance of fasting in the
Christian church? The urgency of this question is what makes
Jesus' words on fasting in Matthew 9:14-17 so important—the
most important in the Bible in my opinion.

The urgency is increased when we consider that in Paul's letters food is celebrated as something good, asceticism is treated as
a weak weapon against fleshly indulgence, and practices of eating and drinking are regarded as nonessential, except as they
express love and contentment in Christ.

The Goodness of Food

In 1 Timothy 4:1-5 Paul warns that in the end times "some will
fall away from the faith . . . and advocate abstaining from
foods." He responds to this attitude toward food by saying,
"God has created [food] to be gratefully shared in by those who
believe and know the truth. For everything created by God is
good, and nothing is to be rejected, if it is received with gratitude;
for it is sanctified by means of the word of God and prayer." So
Paul is eager to warn against a kind of asceticism that exalts fast-

ing in such a way that the goodness of God in the gift of food is overlooked or distorted. Even during the holy times of sharing the Lord's Supper, Paul did not discourage eating, but told the Corinthians to "eat at home, so that you may not come together for judgment" (1 Corinthians 11:34).

The Weakness of Asceticism

And when Paul pondered the value of harsh measures for the body, he cautioned the Colossians that such disciplines are of limited value and can stir up as much carnal pride as they subdue carnal appetite. He fears that the Colossians have drifted away from deep and simple faith in Christ toward external ritual as a means of sanctification: "Why do you submit yourself to decrees, such as, 'Do not handle, *do not taste*, do not touch!' (which all refer to things destined to perish with the using)—in accordance with the commandments and teachings of men?" (Colossians 2:20-22).

What's wrong with these "teachings of men" that call us not to "taste"? He answers, "These are matters which have, to be sure, the appearance of wisdom in self-made religion and *self-abasement and severe treatment of the body*, but are of no value against fleshly indulgence" (Colossians 2:23). This is a strong warning against any simplistic view of fasting that thinks it will automatically do a person spiritual good. It is not that simple. "Severe treatment of the body" may only feed a person's flesh with more self-reliance. C. S. Lewis saw this clearly and sounded the warning:

> Fasting asserts the will against the appetite—the reward being self-mastery and the danger pride: involuntary hunger subjects appetites and will together to the Divine will, furnishing an occasion for submission and exposing us to the

danger of rebellion. But the redemptive effect of suffering lies chiefly in its tendency to reduce the rebel will. Ascetic practices which, in themselves, strengthen the will, are only useful insofar as they enable the will to put its own house (the passions) in order, as a preparation for offering the whole man to God. They are necessary as a means; and as an end, they would be abominable, for in substituting will for appetite and there stopping, they would merely exchange the animal self for the diabolical self. It was therefore truly said that "only God can mortify."[15]

The true mortification of our carnal nature is not a simple matter of denial and discipline. It is an internal, spiritual matter of finding more contentment in Christ than in food.

Eating and Not Eating Are Not Essential

Paul regards eating or not eating as a matter that is nonessential in itself, but which gains value as it expresses love and superior satisfaction in God. Therefore he tells the Roman church, "Let not him who eats regard with contempt him who does not eat, and let not him who does not eat judge him who eats, for God has accepted him. Who are you to judge the servant of another? To his own master he stands or falls; and stand he will, for the Lord is able to make him stand. . . . Let each man be fully convinced in his own mind. . . . He who eats, does so for the Lord, for he gives thanks to God; and he who eats not, for the Lord he does not eat, and gives thanks to God" (Romans 14:3-6).

These words from Romans 14 are not addressed to a situation of fasting. The situation has to do with eating food that some in the church consider taboo because of its associations. But that does not change the principle. Eating and not eating—fasting and not fasting—can both be done "for the Lord" with "thanksgiving to God." Therefore, "let each be fully convinced in his own mind." And, as Paul says in Colossians 2:16, "Let no one act as your judge in regard to food or drink." For "food will not commend us to God; we are neither the worse if we do not eat, nor the better if we do eat" (1 Corinthians 8:8). For "all things are lawful for me, but not all things are profitable. All things are lawful for me, but I will not be mastered by anything" (1 Corinthians 6:12).

The Most Important Word on Fasting in the Bible

So the question demands our attention: Is fasting Christian? If so, how? This is what the words of Jesus in Matthew 9:14-17 ultimately address. That is why they are the most important words on fasting in the Bible. It's time to look at them.

> The disciples of John came to [Jesus], saying, "Why do we and the Pharisees fast, but Your disciples do not fast?" And Jesus said to them, "The attendants of the bridegroom cannot mourn as long as the bridegroom is with them, can they? But the days will come when the bridegroom is taken away from them, and then they will fast. But no one puts a patch of unshrunk cloth on an old garment; for the patch pulls away from the garment, and a worse tear results. Nor do men put new wine into old wineskins; otherwise the wineskins burst, and the wine pours out, and the wineskins are ruined; but they put new wine into fresh wineskins, and both are preserved."

The disciples of John the Baptist come to Jesus and ask why Jesus' disciples don't fast. So evidently Jesus' disciples were not fasting while he was with them. In fact, Jesus had set them an example that earned him the reputation of being anything but an ascetic. When he praised the ministry of John the Baptist he said to the crowds, "John the Baptist has come eating no bread and drinking no wine; and you say, 'He has a demon!' The Son of Man has come *eating and drinking*; and you say, 'Behold, a gluttonous man, and a drunkard, a friend of tax-gatherers and sinners!'" (Luke 7:33-35). In other words, John practiced much fasting, and Jesus practiced little if any (apart from his initial forty-day fast).

Why Didn't Jesus' Disciples Fast?

Now the disciples of John have come to Jesus and want to know why this is. "Why do we and the Pharisees fast, but Your disciples do not fast?" Jesus answers with a word picture. He says, "The attendants of the bridegroom cannot mourn as long as the bridegroom is with them, can they?" With those words Jesus teaches us two things. One is that fasting was, by and large, associated with mourning in that day. It was an expression of brokenheartedness and desperation, usually over sin or over some danger or some deeply longed-for blessing. It was something you did when things were not going the way you wanted them to.

But that's not the situation with the disciples of Jesus. This is the second thing he teaches: the Messiah has come, and his coming is like the coming of a bridegroom to a wedding feast. This, he says, is just too good to mingle with fasting. Jesus was making a tremendous claim for himself here. In the Old Testament God had pictured himself as the husband of his people Israel. "As a young man marries a virgin, so your sons will marry you; and as the bridegroom rejoices over the bride, so your God will rejoice over you" (Isaiah 62:5). "'Then I [the Lord] passed by you [Israel] and saw you, and behold, you were at the time for love; so I spread My skirt over you and covered your nakedness. I also swore to you and entered into a covenant with you so that you became Mine,' declares the Lord GOD" (Ezekiel 16:8). "I [the Lord] will betroth you [Israel] to Me forever; yes,

I will betroth you to Me in righteousness and in justice, in lov-
ingkindness and in compassion, and I will betroth you to Me in
faithfulness. Then you will know the LORD" (Hosea 2:19-20).

Now the Son of God, the Messiah, the long-hoped-for
Prince and Ruler in Israel, has come, and he claims to be the
Bridegroom—that is, the husband of his people—who will be the
true Israel. John the Baptist had recognized this already. When
his disciples asked him about who Jesus was, he said, "You yourselves bear me witness, that I said, 'I am not the Christ,' but, 'I
have been sent before Him.' He who has the bride is the bridegroom; but the friend of the bridegroom, who stands and hears
him, rejoices greatly because of the bridegroom's voice. And so
this joy of mine has been made full" (John 3:28-29).

John's partially-veiled claim is the kind Jesus made about his
identity with God. If you had ears to hear, you could hear it. God,
the one who betrothed Israel to himself in covenant love, has
come.

This is so stunning and so glorious and so unexpected in
this form that Jesus said, you simply cannot fast now in this situation. It is too happy and too spectacularly exhilarating.
Fasting is for times of yearning and aching and longing. But the
bridegroom of Israel is here. After a thousand years of dream-
ing and longing and hoping and waiting, he is here! The absence
of fasting in the band of disciples was a witness to the presence
of God in their midst.

When Will the Disciples Fast?

But then Jesus said, "The days will come when the bridegroom
is taken away from them, and then they will fast." This is the key
sentence: "*Then they will fast.*" When is he referring to?

Some have suggested that he was referring only to the several days between his death and resurrection. In other words, the

Bridegroom will be taken away from Good Friday through Easter Sunday morning. During those three days the disciples would fast. But then he would be with them again, and they would not fast any longer. Support for this view is found in John 16:22-23 where Jesus predicts his death and resurrection with these words: "You too now have sorrow; but I will see you again, and your heart will rejoice, and no one takes your joy away from you. And in that day you will ask Me no question. Truly, truly, I say to you, if you shall ask the Father for anything, He will give it to you in My name." In other words, after the resurrection, during the church age, there will be indestructible joy among Christ's disciples. Does this mean that fasting is excluded? Is Jesus only prophesying that his disciples would fast between Good Friday and Easter?

That is very unlikely for several reasons. One is that, for all its joy, the early church fasted on certain occasions (Acts 13:1-3; 14:23; 2 Corinthians 6:5; 11:27). Therefore the earliest Christians did not take Jesus' words to mean that fasting would be excluded after the resurrection.

What then does Jesus mean when he says, "The days will come when the bridegroom is taken away from them, and then they will fast"? He means that after his death and resurrection he will return to his Father in heaven, and during that time the disciples will fast. Robert Gundry is right when he says, "The entirety of the church age constitutes 'the days' that 'will come when the bridegroom is taken away.'"[16] In my judgment, the strongest reason for this view is that the only other place in Matthew where Jesus uses this term "bridegroom" is to refer to himself coming back at the end of the church age. In Matthew 25:1-13 Jesus pictures his second coming as the arrival of the bridegroom. "At midnight there was a shout, 'Behold, the bridegroom! Come out to meet him'" (verse 6). So Jesus clearly thinks of himself as a bridegroom who is gone not only for three days between Good Friday and Easter, but for all the time until the second coming. This is the time he has in mind when he says, "Then they will fast"—until the second coming.

Arthur Wallis is justified in entitling the sixth chapter of his book, *God's Chosen Fast*, "The Time Is Now."[17] Now is when Jesus says his disciples will fast. He is saying: Now while I am here in your midst as the bridegroom you cannot fast, but I am not going to remain with you. There will come a time when I return to my Father in heaven. And during that time you will fast. That time is now.

It is true that Jesus has given the Holy Spirit in his absence, and that the Holy Spirit is "the Spirit of Jesus" (Acts 16:7; 2 Corinthians 3:17). So in a profound and wonderful sense Jesus is still with us. He said, speaking of the "Comforter," the Spirit, "I will not leave you as orphans; I will come to you" (John 14:18). Nevertheless, there is a greater degree of intimacy that we will enjoy with Christ in heaven when this age is over. So in another sense Christ is *not* with us, but away from us. This is why Paul said in 2 Corinthians 5:8 "We [would] prefer to be absent from the body and *at home with the Lord*," and in Philippians 1:23, "*To depart and be with Christ* . . . is very much better." In other words, in this age there is an ache inside every Christian that Jesus is not here as fully and intimately and as powerfully and as gloriously as we want him to be. We hunger for so much more. That is why we fast.

Is Fasting the Old Wineskin That Has to Go?

But then Jesus says something very crucial in Matthew 9:16-17. He puts together two images, one about patched garments, and the other about worn-out wineskins. "But no one puts a patch of unshrunk cloth on an old garment; for the patch pulls away from the garment, and a worse tear results. Nor do men put new wine into old wineskins; otherwise the wineskins burst, and the wine pours out, and the wineskins are ruined; but they put new wine into fresh wineskins, and both are preserved."

The patch of unshrunk cloth and the new wine represent the new reality that has come with Jesus—the Kingdom of God is here. The Bridegroom has come. The Messiah is in our midst. And that is not temporary. He is not here and then gone. The kingdom of God did not come in Jesus and then just vanish out of the world. Jesus died for our sins once for all. He rose from the dead once for all. The Spirit was sent into the world as the real presence of Jesus among us. The kingdom of God is the present reigning power of Christ in the world subduing hearts to the King and creating a people who believe him and serve him in faith and holiness. The Spirit of the bridegroom is gathering and purifying a bride for Christ. This is the gospel of Christ and "the mystery of the kingdom" that we referred to above.[18] This is the new wine.

And Jesus says the old wineskins can't contain it. Something has to change. What is the old wineskin? In the context, we can't escape the connection with fasting. There is no break in Jesus' thought. Follow it from verse 15 to 16: "The days will come when the bridegroom is taken away from them, and then they will fast. But no one puts a patch of unshrunk cloth on an old garment. . . ." There is no break. And this is true in all three Gospels where this account is recorded. The old shrunken patch of cloth and the old brittle wineskins relate directly to fasting as an old Jewish custom.

Fasting was inherited from the Old Testament and had been used as part of the Jewish system of relating to God. In Luke 18:11-12 we get a glimpse of this old practice as the Pharisee prays, "God, I thank Thee that I am not like other people: swindlers, unjust, adulterers, or even like this tax-gatherer. *I fast twice a week*; I pay tithes of all that I get." This traditional fasting is the old wineskin. And Jesus says that it cannot contain the new wine of the kingdom that he is bringing.

Now this presents us with a problem. In Matthew 9:15 Jesus says that we will fast when the Bridegroom is gone. And two verses later he says that the old fasting cannot contain the new wine of the kingdom. In other words, Jesus' disciples *will* fast; but the fasting they have known is not suitable for the new reality of his presence and the inbreaking kingdom of God.

New Wine Calls for New Fasting

What then shall we say? Are we to fast as Christians, or are we not? Is fasting Christian, or isn't it? I believe the answer is that the new wine of Christ's presence demands not *no* fasting, but *new* fasting. Years ago I wrote in the margin of my Greek Testament beside Matthew 9:17, "The new fasting is based on the mystery that the bridegroom *has* come, not just *will* come. The new wine of his presence calls for new fasting."

In other words, the yearning and longing and ache of the *old* fasting was not based on the glorious truth that the Messiah had come. The mourning over sin and the yearning for deliverance from danger and the longing for God that inspired the old fasting were not based on the great finished work of the Redeemer and the great revelation of his truth and grace in history. These things were all still in the future. But now the Bridegroom has come. And in coming he struck the decisive blow against sin and Satan and death.

What distinguishes Christianity from Judaism is that the longed-for kingdom of God is now present as well as future. The King has come. "The kingdom of God has come upon you" (Luke 11:20). "The kingdom of God is in your midst" (Luke 17:21). It is true that the kingdom of God is not yet fully consummated. It is still to come in glorious fullness and power. At the Last Supper Jesus said, "I will not drink of the fruit of the vine from now on *until the kingdom of God comes*" (Luke 22:18). So it is plain that the kingdom of God is still a future reality yet to come, even though Jesus said that "the kingdom of God has come upon you" and "is in your midst" (which is why George Ladd's book is entitled *The Presence of the Future*[19]).

This is the Center referred to earlier, which fasting has to relate to if it is going to be Christian. The Center is the decisive triumph of the Son of God, the Messiah, entering history and dying and rising from the dead and reigning over history for the salvation of his people and the glory of his Father. Christians are a people captured by a great hope that one day they will see and be enthralled by the fullness of the glory of God in Christ. But what is decisively Christian in this is that our hope is rooted in the past historical triumph of that very God over sin and death and hell by the death and resurrection of Jesus.[20] Christianity is a vibrant hope for the consummation of history in the universal manifestation of the glory of God in Christ—a hope that is unshakably rooted in the past incarnation of Christ who offered himself once for all as a sacrifice for sin and sat down at the right hand of God (Hebrews 10:12). This is the new wine.

The great, central, decisive act of salvation for us today is past, not future. And on the basis of that past work of the Bridegroom, nothing can ever be the same again. The Lamb is slain. The blood is shed. The punishment of our sins is executed. Death is defeated. The Spirit is sent. The wine is new. And the old fasting mindset is simply not adequate.

The Newness of the New Fasting

What then is new about the new *Christian* fasting? What's new about Christian fasting is that it rests on all this finished work of the Bridegroom. It assumes that. It believes that. It enjoys that. The aching and yearning and longing for Christ and his power that drive us to fasting are not the expression of empti- ness. Need, yes. Pain, yes. Hunger for God, yes. But not empti- ness. The firstfruits of what we long for have already come. The downpayment of what we yearn for is already paid. The fullness that we are longing for and fasting for has appeared in history, and we have beheld his glory. It is not merely future. We do not fast out of emptiness. Christ is already in us the hope of glory (Colossians 1:27). We have been "sealed . . . with the Holy Spirit of promise, who is given [now!] as a pledge of our inheritance" (Ephesians 1:13-14; see also 2 Corinthians 1:22; 5:5).

We have tasted the powers of the age to come, and our fasting is not because we are hungry for something we have not experienced, but because the new wine of Christ's presence is so real and so satisfying. We must have all that it is possible to have. The newness of our fasting is this: its intensity comes not because we have never tasted the wine of Christ's presence, but because we have tasted it so wonderfully by his Spirit, and can- not now be satisfied until the consummation of joy arrives. The new fasting, the *Christian* fasting, is a hunger for all the fullness of God (Ephesians 3:19), aroused by the aroma of Jesus' love and by the taste of God's goodness in the gospel of Christ (1 Peter 2:2-3).

The Fasting That Is Feasting

Another way to say it is that the new fasting is the fasting of *faith*. Faith stands on the finished work of Christ and, on that foundation, becomes the "assurance of things hoped for" (Hebrews 11:1). Faith is a spiritual feasting on Christ with a view to being so satisfied in him that the power of all other allurements is broken.[21] This feasting begins by receiving the past grace of Christ's death and resurrection, and then embraces all that God promises to be for us in him. As long as we are finite and fallen, Christian faith will mean both delighting in the (past) incarnation and desiring the (future) consummation. It will be both contentment and dissatisfaction. And the dissatisfaction will grow directly out of the measure of contentment that we have known in Christ.

Fasting Does Belong in the Kingdom of God

This understanding of Christian fasting answers all the concerns raised earlier by Keith Main. He said that "the prayer life of the New Testament is a sign of the inbreaking of the kingdom of God. Fasting is no longer consistent with the joyous and thankful attitude that marks the fellowship."[22] We see now that this is an overstatement. Yes, the kingdom has broken in. Yes, there is a deep drinking even now on the end-time glory manifest in Christ and experienced by his Spirit. But, no, this is not so full and uninterrupted that aching and longing and desiring are completely overcome.

Even Main himself backs off and admits this when he says,

It is true that the crisis and the tragedy are there as a stark reality. The Kingdom is not *fully* realized. Granted that the Bridegroom is present and now is not an appropriate time to mourn. Yet this is not entirely so, for we are still in the flesh and weak in faith. . . . Within this "bitter struggle" the believer, in his devotional life, might conceivably find occasion to fast. It would be only one among many of the ingredients that go to make up the life of the man in Christ.[23]

That's right. The presence of the Bridegroom through his Spirit, in the triumph of forgiveness and fellowship, does not make fasting negligible, it makes it new.

Fasting as an Expression of Dissatisfied Contentment

As an act of faith, Christian fasting is an expression of dissatisfied contentment in the all-sufficiency of Christ. It is an expression of secure and happy longing for the all-satisfying fullness of Christ. Christian fasting does not tremble in the hope of earning anything from Christ. It looks away from itself to the final payment of Calvary for every blessing it will ever receive. Christian fasting is not self-wrought discipline that tries to deserve more from God. It is a hunger for God awakened by the taste of God freely given in the gospel.

Christian Fasting Affirms the Goodness of Food

This is why the warnings we raised earlier from Paul's letters are not really objections against Christian fasting, but only against its distortions. "God has created [food] to be gratefully shared in by those who believe and know the truth. For everything created by God is good, and nothing is to be rejected, if it is received with gratitude; for it is sanctified by means of the word of God and prayer" (1 Timothy 4:3-5). Paul's praise for the goodness of food, and for the freedom that Christians have to enjoy it, is not a contradiction of Christian fasting. The Christian says yes to every good and perfect gift that comes down from the Father of lights (James 1:17).

Fasting is not a no to the goodness of food or the generosity of God in providing it. Rather, it is a way of saying, from time to time, that having more of the Giver surpasses having the gift. If a husband and wife resolve to give up sexual relations for a season to deal earnestly with a problem keeping them at odds, this is not a condemnation of sex but an exaltation of love. Food is good. But God is better. Normally we meet God in his good gifts and turn every enjoyment into worship with thanksgiving. But from time to time we need to test ourselves to see if we have begun to love his gifts in place of God.

Christian Fasting Is Not "Willpower Religion"

The great danger Paul saw in self-made and self-exalting fasting does not nullify the new Christian fasting. Paul warns that there is a fasting that is a "self-made religion and [a] self-abasement and severe treatment of the body, [but has] no value against fleshly indulgence" (Colossians 2:23). In other words, this fasting is a "willpower religion"[24] that actually stirs up the spiritual pride of the flesh even while mastering its physical appetites.

But this is the exact opposite of Christian fasting. Christian fasting moves from broken and contrite poverty of spirit to sweet satisfaction in the free mercy of Christ to ever greater desires and enjoyments of God's inexhaustible grace. Christian fasting does not bolster pride, because it rests with childlike contentment in the firmly accomplished justification of God in Christ, even while longing for all the fullness of God possible in this life. Christian fasting is the effect of what Christ has already done *for* us and *in* us. It is not our feat, but the Spirit's fruit. Recall that the last-mentioned fruit of the Spirit is "self-control"[25] (Galatians 5:23).

All Eating Is Lawful, but Not All Is Helpful

What all this means for Paul's practice is that he was free to fast or not to fast. "All things are lawful for me, but not all things are profitable. All things are lawful for me, but I will not be mastered by anything" (1 Corinthians 6:12). The reason for this is that the act of fasting was not the essential thing. Doing it—or not doing it—for the glory of God was the essential thing: "He who eats, does so for the Lord, for he gives thanks to God; and he who eats

not, *for the Lord he does not eat, and gives thanks to God*"
(Romans 14:6). Fasting gives glory to God when it is experienced
as a gift from God aimed at knowing and enjoying more of God.
God is glorified in us when we aim our behavior at being most
satisfied in him. We may do this by grateful eating or by grateful
fasting. His gifts leave a hunger for him beyond themselves, and
fasting from his gifts puts that hunger to the test.

Should a Christian Buffet the Body?

It is misleading, without careful qualification, to say (as Keith
Main does) that "Paul . . . deliberately diverted the disciples'
attention away from fasting and any form of food asceticism
and into prayer, service, and toil on behalf of the kingdom."[26]
I agree with the positive second half of this statement, not the
negative first half. I would say Paul *did* direct our attention
toward fasting and numerous other kinds of self-denial—*not* as
meritorious religious rituals, and not as an end in themselves,
but as a weapon in the fight of faith. Twice, when Paul was list-
ing his trials, he mentioned fasting. "I have been in labor and
hardship, through many sleepless nights, in hunger and thirst,
often in fastings,[27] in cold and exposure" (2 Corinthians 11:27;
see also 6:5).

　　　This fits with what he said about how he handled the
appetites of his body. "*I buffet my body and make it my slave,*
lest possibly, after I have preached to others, I myself should be
disqualified" (1 Corinthians 9:26-27). I take this to mean that
Paul regarded some ascetic discipline as a useful weapon in the
fight of faith. Holding fast to Christ *by faith* is the key to not
being "disqualified." This is plain, for example, from Colossians
1:23, "[Christ will present you holy and blameless to God] if
indeed you *continue in the faith* firmly established and steadfast,

and *not moved away from the hope* of the gospel." Persevering *faith* is the key to standing before God acceptable in the last day.

Paul says that one weapon in this ongoing fight of faith is the practice of "buffeting the body." He was not unaware that the desires of the body are deceitful as well as delightful. He said that the "old self" is "being corrupted in accordance with the *desires of deceit*" (Ephesians 4:22, author's translation). The nature of this deceit is to lure us subtly into living for the "fleeting pleasures" of body and mind, rather than the spiritual delights of knowing and serving God. These pleasures start as innocent delights in food and reading and resting and playing, but then become ends in themselves and choke off spiritual hunger for God. Paul buffets his body to put himself to the test. Does he hunger for God? Is his faith real? Or is he becoming the slave of comfort and bodily pleasures? You can hear the passion of his heart in 1 Corinthians 6:12, "I will not be mastered by anything!" This is not the pride of Stoic self-exaltation. It is the passionate resolve to resist anything that lures the heart away from an all-controlling satisfaction in God.

When I was preaching on fasting and prayer some years ago, a young man came up to me after one of the messages and told me a story that illustrates the kind of buffeting the body in prayer that fits a person for heaven. I had referred to the South Korean church as pacesetters in this regard. That moved the young man to talk to me after the service.

I grew up on the mission field in Korea. There is one experience emblazoned on my mind to show the sacrificial dedication to prayer and fasting in Korea. My father worked with a leper colony, and they had prayer meetings that met at four o'clock in the morning. I was a little boy, but my father took me with him, getting me up at about 3:30 A.M. to get there on time. He sat me down in the back where I could see out the door. And I'll never forget one man who had no legs, no crutches, and was using his hands and crabbing along the ground, dragging his body to pray at 4 A.M. I'll never forget that.

Rising early is a kind of fast. And coming to pray when it is hard to get there is another kind of fast. When we make such choices, we make war on the deceitfulness of our desires and declare the preciousness of prayer and the all-surpassing worth of God.

Is Fasting Christian?

Is fasting Christian? It is if it comes from confidence in Christ and is sustained by the power of Christ and aims at the glory of Christ. Over every Christian fast should be written the words, "I count all things to be loss in view of the surpassing value of knowing Christ Jesus my Lord, for whom I have suffered the loss of all things, and count them but rubbish in order that I may gain Christ" (Philippians 3:7-8). In fasting, as well as in all other privations, every loss is for the sake of "gaining Christ." But this does not mean that we seek to gain a Christ we do not have. Nor does it mean that our progress depends on ourselves. Four verses later Paul makes plain the dynamics of the entire Christian life—including fasting: "I press on in order that I may lay hold of that for which also I was laid hold of by Christ Jesus."

This is the essence of Christian fasting: We ache and yearn—and fast—to know more and more of all that God is for us in Jesus. But only because he has already laid hold of us and is drawing us ever forward and upward into "all the fullness of God."

My prayer for the Christian church is that God might

awaken in us a new hunger for himself—a new fasting. Not because we haven't tasted the new wine of Christ's presence, but because we *have* tasted it and long, with a deep and joyful aching of soul, to know more of his presence and power in our midst.

And you shall remember all the way
which the LORD your God has led you
in the wilderness these forty years
that He might humble you, testing you,
to know what was in your heart,
whether you would keep His commandments or not.
And He humbled you and let you be hungry,
and fed you with manna which you did not know,
nor did your fathers know,
that He might make you understand
that man does not live by bread alone,
but man lives by everything
that proceeds out of the mouth of the LORD.

—DEUTERONOMY 8:2-3

The weakness of hunger which leads to death brings forth the goodness and power of God who wills life. Here there is no extortion, no magic attempt to force God's will. We merely look with confidence upon our heavenly Father and through our fasting say gently in our hearts: "Father, without you I will die; come to my assistance, make haste to help me."

—JOSEPH WIMMER
Fasting in the New Testament[1]

2

MAN SHALL NOT LIVE
BY BREAD ALONE

---

*The Desert Feast
of Fasting*

The Son of God began his earthly ministry with a forty-day fast. This should give us pause. Especially if we—who are not God—have moved into ministry heedless of the battle we may have to fight. Why did Jesus do this? Why did God lead him to it? And what about us? Can we really face the superhuman hazards of life and ministry without walking with Jesus through the wilderness of fasting?

I think we must walk there to learn from him, at least, if not to imitate his triumph. He *was* the Son of God, and we are not. But he did say, "As the Father has sent Me, I also send you" (John 20:21). The salvation of the world may not hang on our success, since we are light-years less than he. But that may heighten rather than lessen the need of fasting in our lives. The stakes of *my* warfare are smaller for the world, but my weakness is greater. Why did he fast as he began his great work? What can we learn about our own?

Hungry for All the Fullness of God

My heart is hungry for "all the fullness of God." I long for a deeper work of God in the midst of his people. I yearn for a mighty tide of missionary zeal to spread a passion for the supremacy of Christ in all things for the joy of all peoples. I long to see unmistakable, supernatural new birth taking place week in and week out through the compelling witness of God's transformed people wherever he is named. The ministry of Jesus was, and always will be, unparalleled. In some measure, it is a model for us. But in its fullness it bears witness to his utter divine uniqueness. Yet how can we not wonder if this extraordinary fast at the beginning of his ministry was meant for more than his own work?

Charles Spurgeon, the London pastor from a century ago, said, "Our seasons of fasting and prayer at the Tabernacle have been high days indeed; never has Heaven's gate stood wider; never have our hearts been nearer the central Glory."[2] Getting near the glory of God is surely the key to burning with inextinguishable light and heat. And is this not the need of the hour—every hour—that the blind may see, and turn from darkness to light, and give glory to our Father in heaven (Acts 26:18; Matthew 5:16)? If he who was *the* Light of the world fought for his fire with fasting, is there something to be learned here for our flickering wicks?

The Spirit Descended on Jesus Like a Dove

I think there is. Let us go back, then, and learn from him. According to Matthew 3:16, after being baptized, Jesus came up out of the water and the heavens opened and the Holy Spirit descended on him like a dove. What does this mean? The Holy Spirit had always been with Jesus. He was conceived by the Holy

Spirit in his virgin mother's womb (Luke 1:35). And for all eternity before that, the Son of God and the Spirit of God had been one, as Paul said so bluntly, "The Lord is the Spirit" (2 Corinthians 3:17). What then does Matthew mean when he reports that "the heavens were opened, and [Jesus] saw the Spirit of God descending as a dove, and coming upon Him"?

He means that God the Father so loved his Son that he would publicly and powerfully prepare him in this special way for the ministry that lay before him. He would assure him of his favor and his guidance and his sustaining help. As the Spirit comes upon Jesus, God the Father says (in verse 17), "This is my beloved Son, in whom I am well pleased." In other words, this special manifestation of the Spirit was a demonstration of the Father's infinite love for his Son ("This is my *loved* son"), and the Father's great endorsement of his person and ministry ("in whom I am well pleased").

None Had Ever Ventured Such a Thing, Nor Could They

What Jesus was about to undertake is unique in the history of the world. No other man ever set his face to live and die as "the Lamb of God who takes away the sin of the world" (John 1:29). Jesus knew that his task as the Son of Man was "to give his life a ransom for many" (Mark 10:45), and that he "came into the world to save sinners" (1 Timothy 1:15). He knew from Isaiah 53 that it was the will of God to crush him, and to lay on him the iniquity of us all, and by his death to justify many sinners (verses 6, 10-11). He knew that God had passed over many sins in former days, and that the vindication of the justice of God was at stake in his life and ministry (Romans 3:25-26). He knew that God's truthfulness in all his promises rode on Jesus' faithful and obedient fulfillment of every word spoken in the Old Testament (Romans 15:8). He knew that all this would cost him his life and that the torture would be unspeakably shameful and painful (Mark 10:33-34).

The Father knew this was coming, and the Son knew it was coming. And so the Father commissions the Spirit to fly like a dove upon the Son to assure him of the Father's love and to make manifest beyond all question the approval of the Father. One of the wonderful effects of the Father's words, "My beloved Son in whom I am well pleased," is to assure Jesus—and us—that the fire of misery that Jesus was walking into was *not* owing to his Father's displeasure. Already the Father was preparing Jesus—and us—to know that the desperate cry, "Why hast thou forsaken me?" would not be the last word.

The Spirit Leads Jesus into Testing and Fasting

This is especially important to see when we notice in the next verse (Matthew 4:1) what the Spirit's first act is after coming upon Jesus in this way. It says, "Then Jesus was led up by the Spirit into the wilderness to be tempted by the devil." The first act of the Spirit in Jesus' ministry was to lead him into the wilderness and to expose him to Satan's testings.

Under the Spirit's leading Jesus prepared himself for this testing by fasting. "Jesus was led up by the Spirit into the wilderness to be tempted by the devil. *And after He had fasted forty days . . .*" The Spirit of God willed that the Son of God be tested on his way into the ministry, and he willed that Jesus triumph in this testing through fasting. It must not go unnoticed that Jesus triumphed over the great enemy of his soul and our salvation through fasting.

It seems to me that this story should shake us. Here is Jesus, standing on the threshold of the most important ministry in the history of the world. On his obedience and righteousness hangs the salvation of the world. None will escape damnation without this ministry of obedient suffering and death and resurrection. And God wills that, at the very outset, this ministry be threatened with destruction—namely, the temptations of Satan to abandon the path of lowliness and suffering and obedience. And of all the hundreds of things Jesus might have done to fight off this tremendous threat to salvation, he is led, in the Spirit, to fast.

If Satan had succeeded in deterring Jesus from the path of humble, sacrificial obedience, there would be no salvation. We would still be in our sins and without hope. Therefore, we owe our salvation, in some measure (not to overstate it), to the fasting of Jesus. This is a remarkable tribute to fasting. Don't pass over this quickly. Think on it. Jesus began his ministry with fasting. And he triumphed over his enemy through fasting. And our salvation was accomplished through perseverance by fasting.

The Reenactment of Israel's Testing in the Wilderness

Now to see the fuller meaning of this, we must look at the book of Deuteronomy. Each time Jesus responded to the three temptations of the devil in the wilderness he quoted from Deuteronomy. "Man shall not live by bread alone"— Deuteronomy 8:3. "You shall not tempt the Lord your God"— Deuteronomy 6:16. "You shall worship the Lord your God and him only shall you serve"—Deuteronomy 6:13.

This is very significant. Here is Jesus led by the Spirit into the wilderness—mark this, the *wilderness* — and to counter the temptations of Satan, Jesus quotes passages from Deuteronomy, all of which are spoken by Moses to the people of Israel about their time of *testing in the wilderness*.

Matthew 4:3-4 says, "The tempter came and said to Him, 'If You are the Son of God, command that these stones become bread.' But He answered and said, 'It is written, Man shall not live on bread alone, but on every word that proceeds out of the

mouth of God.'" Now compare Deuteronomy 8:2-3, and notice
the parallels between that situation in the wilderness and Jesus'
situation in the wilderness. Moses says to the people,

> You shall remember all the way which the Lord your God
> has led you in the wilderness [note: as Jesus was led by the
> Spirit in the wilderness] these forty years [note: as Jesus was
> there forty days], that He might humble you, testing you
> [note: as Jesus was "tested"], to know what was in your
> heart, whether you would keep His commandments or not.
> And He humbled you and let you be hungry [note: as Jesus
> was made hungry by his fasting], and fed you with manna
> which you did not know, nor did your fathers know, that He
> might make you understand that man does not live by bread
> alone, but man lives by everything that proceeds out of the
> mouth of the Lord [note: just as Jesus says to Satan].

There are too many similarities between what is happening
to Jesus here in the wilderness and what happened to the people
of Israel to think it is a mere coincidence. God is teaching us
something here. The Spirit of God led Jesus into the wilderness.
What does this mean?

It means that Old Testament shadows are being replaced
with New Testament reality. It means that something greater than
Moses and the wilderness and the Law and Joshua and the
Promised Land is at stake here. It means that the time of fulfillment is at hand. The promise to Moses is coming true. "The
LORD your God will raise up for you a prophet like me from
among you, from your countrymen, you shall listen to him"
(Deuteronomy 18:15). It means that God is now, with the incarnation of his Son, preparing to deliver his people—the new
Israel—from the Egyptian bondage of sin into the Promised Land
of forgiveness and righteousness and eternal life. To do this he has
sent a new Moses, or in this case, a new Joshua (Jesus reenacts

both roles, and the name "Jesus" is identical to "Joshua" in New Testament Greek). This new Joshua stands as the head and representative of the whole new people that Jesus will gather from Jews and Gentiles. On their behalf Jesus will now be led by the Spirit into the wilderness. He will stay forty days to represent forty years. He will be tested as Israel was tested. And he will hunger as Israel hungered. And if he triumphs, he and all his people go safely into the Promised Land of forgiveness and eternal life.

His Fasting Was Both War and Weapon, Testing and Triumph

Now we can see the meaning of Jesus' fasting more clearly. It was not an arbitrary choice of something to do in the face of Satanic temptation. It was a voluntary act of identification with the people of God in their wilderness deprivation and trial. Jesus was saying in effect, "I have been sent to lead the people of God out of the bondage of sin into the Promised Land of salvation. To do this I must be one of them. That is why I was born. That is why I was baptized. Therefore I will take on the testing that they experienced. I will represent them in the wilderness and allow my heart to be probed with fasting to see where my allegiance is and who is my God. And, with the Spirit's help, I will triumph through this fasting. I will overcome the devil and lead all who trust me into the Promised Land of eternal glory."

In other words, Jesus' fasting was not only preparation for testing, it was part of his testing, in the same way that hunger was a test of faith for the people of Israel in the wilderness. Moses said, "[God led you in the wilderness] that He might humble you, testing you, to know what was in your heart, whether you would keep His commandments or not. And He humbled you and let you be hungry" (Deuteronomy 8:2). So it was with Jesus. The Spirit led him in the wilderness and let him be hungry that he might test him to see what was in his heart. Did he love God or did he love bread? But that doesn't mean that his fasting was not also—even at the same time—a weapon in the fight against Satan. Fasting tests where the heart is. And when it reveals that the heart is with God and not the world, a mighty blow is struck against Satan. For then Satan does not have the foothold he would if our heart were in love with earthly things like bread.

Fasting as a Heart-revealing Forfeiture

The people of God are often called to go without the ordinary means of life. "Many are the afflictions of the righteous" (Psalm 34:19). "Through many tribulations we must enter the kingdom" (Acts 14:22). "Even we ourselves groan . . . waiting the redemption of our bodies" (Romans 8:23). Fasting is a brief, voluntary experience of this deprivation. When we experience this willing forfeiture, the Lord reveals what is in our hearts. What are we controlled by? What do we value and trust? We saw this already in the Introduction and referred there to Richard Foster's comment in *The Celebration of Discipline* that "more than any other discipline, fasting reveals the things that control us."[3]

What are we slaves to? What are we most hungry for—food or God? Fasting is God's testing ground—and healing ground. Will we murmur as the Israelites murmured in the absence of bread? For Jesus the question was: Would he leave the path of sacrificial obedience and turn stones into bread? Or would he "live by every word that proceeds out of the mouth of God"? Fasting is a way of revealing to ourselves and confessing to our God what is in our hearts. Where do we find our deepest satisfaction—in God or in his gifts?

And the aim of fasting is that we come to rely less on food and more on God. That's the meaning of the words in Matthew 4:4, "Man shall not live on bread alone, but on every word that proceeds out of the mouth of God." Every time we fast we are saying with Jesus, "Not by bread alone, but by you, Lord. Not by bread alone, but by you, Lord."

Fasting for God, Not His Miracle Bread

Let me try to show you why I think this is what Jesus means when he repels Satan with the words, "[Man shall live] on every word that proceeds out of the mouth of God." Why do I think Jesus is saying, "Trust in God, not in bread"?

The key is found in the context of Deuteronomy 8:3 where Jesus gets the word in Matthew 4:4:

> [God] fed you with manna which you did not know, nor did your fathers know, that [note the argument] He might make you understand that man does not live by bread alone, but man lives by everything that proceeds out of the mouth of the Lord.

Notice carefully. Now he is saying that the giving of manna is the test. Not the *withholding* of food, but the *giving* of food— to teach them that man does not live by bread alone. He gave them manna, an utterly unheard-of food falling from heaven. Why? So that they would learn, Moses says, to live on everything that comes from the mouth of God. Now how is that? How does the giving of miraculous manna teach that? Because manna is one of the incredible ways God can, with a mere word, meet your needs when all else looks hopeless. So Moses' point is that we must learn to depend on God and not ourselves. We must trust him for every utterly unexpected blessing that is commanded for us from the mouth of God.

But now watch what Satan does with that truth in dealing with Jesus. Satan says to Jesus, "If you are the Son of God, command these stones to become bread" (Matthew 4:3). In other words, "Make manna for yourself, like your Father did in the wilderness." Satan is crafty in the extreme. He is a subtle exegete of Scripture. He knows the raw content of the Bible. He has seen that the manna was meant to teach the miracle-working power of God to provide for his people in distress. So he argues with Jesus, "The reason your Father gave manna in the wilderness was to teach the people to expect miracles in distress; so treat yourself to some miracle bread, and you will be obeying Scripture."

To this Jesus responds, "Satan, you are so close and yet so far. You have always handled the word of God that way, so subtly and so deceptively. You sound like you approve, but you turn every word against God. The point of the manna was this, Satan: Don't trust in bread—nor even miracle bread—trust in *God*! Don't get your deepest satisfactions in life from food—not even God-wrought miracle food—but from God. Every word that comes out of the mouth of God reveals God. And it is this self-revelation that we feed on most deeply. This will last for ever. This is eternal life. Be gone, Satan, *God* is my portion. I will not turn from his path and his fellowship, not even for miraculous manna."

This is the deepest lesson of Jesus' fasting in the wilderness. It was a weapon in the war against satanic deception because it was a demonstration that Jesus hungered more for God and God's will than he did for God's wonders. He might have rationalized that turning stones to bread is precisely what the Son of God should do as he reenacted the wilderness experience of God's people. They got manna. He would get manna. In that case, fasting would be a religious prelude to miraculous provision.

But that is not how Jesus reasoned. And that is not what fasting was. Instead, Jesus reasoned like this: "I have been sent to suffer and to die for my people. The only hope of carrying this through is to so love God, my Father, that he is more precious to me than even the demonstrations of his miraculous power to relieve me of my distresses. I know it is his will to crush me and put me to grief for the sake of his people. I have read it in Isaiah 53:10. I will not use fasting as an effort to escape this calling. That is what Satan wants me to make of it— a prelude to the miraculous divine provision of bread, just like Deuteronomy. But here's the difference. They were tested a little, and I will be tested much. For much more hangs on my test than on theirs."

The Triumph of Hunger for God

And what then was fasting for Jesus? It was both test and triumph. It was the test of his deepest appetite and the triumph of his hunger for God above all things. And therefore it was also a triumph over Satan. The Calvary Road was the way to his own death and the defeat of the devil. At the cross Jesus "disarmed the rulers and authorities [and] made a public display of them, having triumphed over them" (Colossians 2:15). The road that led to this defeat started with a forty-day fast. And in that fast Jesus demonstrated the power that enabled him to bruise the serpent's head at Golgotha. It was the power of faith, that is, the power of a superior satisfaction in God above all things, even the miraculous gifts of God. This deep confidence and contentment in God sustained Christ all the way to the end. *"For the joy set before Him* [Christ] endured the cross, despising the shame, and has sat down at the right hand of the throne of God" (Hebrews 12:2).

Fasting is a periodic—and sometimes decisive—declaration that we would rather feast at God's table in the kingdom of heaven than feed on the finest delicacies of this world. Jesus knew what he had left in heaven. And he knew what he was returning to. This was his great hope and joy. He once said to his disciples. "If you loved Me, you would have rejoiced, because I go to the Father; for the Father is greater than I" (John 14:28). To return to the Father with "the fruit of the travail of his soul"—the church—(Isaiah 53:11, RSV) was Jesus' great desire. On this his soul feasted, and this is what sustained him in fasting and dying.

Can We Do Without the Hungry Handmaid of Faith?

The question for us is not mainly whether we fast, but whether we hunger for God like this. Is this the nature of our faith—that we are satisfied with all God promises to be for us in Jesus? So satisfied that we can take up our cross and follow him on the Calvary Road? So hungry for him alone that not even the wonders and miracles of his provision are sufficient to satisfy our souls? And if that is the question, then we must ask, Can we do without the hungry handmaid of faith called fasting?

The question is not of earning or meriting or coercing anything from God. The question is: having tasted the goodness of God in the gospel, how can I maximize my enjoyment of him, when every moment of my life I am tempted to make a god out of his good gifts? By what weapons shall I fight the fight of faith and guard my heart from alien affections and treasonous appetites? Surely I will take the sword of the Spirit, the Word of God, and I will pray. But I will also take the poor and hungry handmaid of faith as my help. In her weakness she is strong. Her emptiness magnifies my need and makes the perfection of God more precious.

> The weakness of hunger which leads to death brings forth the goodness and power of God who wills life. Here there is no extortion, no magic attempt to force God's will. We merely look with confidence upon our heavenly Father and through

our fasting say gently in our hearts: "Father, without you I will die; come to my assistance, make haste to help me."[4]

How Shall We Sustain a Soul-satisfying Vision of God?

The assistance we need, above all physical healing and all financial security and all employment successes and all career guidance and all relational harmony, is the divine assistance to see and to savor the glory of God in Christ. Beholding the glory of God in the gospel, we were saved (2 Corinthians 4:4,6). Beholding the glory of God in his promises, we are being sanctified (2 Corinthians 3:18). There is only one way that we will finish our course and keep the faith and persevere to the end, and that is by "fixing our eyes on Jesus" (Hebrews 12:2; see also 3:1), and by looking "not at the things which are seen, but at the things which are not seen" (2 Corinthians 4:18), and by setting "[our] minds on things that are above" (Colossians 3:2). This is God's will for us and God's work in us (Hebrews 13:20-21). But we are so constituted as fallen human beings, Jesus says, that "the deceitfulness of riches, and the desires for other things [even innocent things like food] enter in and choke the word," which is meant to reveal to us the glory of God (Mark 4:19). Therefore the fight of faith and the battle to behold the glory of the Lord day by day is fought not only by feeding the soul on truth, but fasting, to put our appetites to the test, and if necessary to death.

Dietrich Bonhoeffer wrestled earnestly with "The Cost of Discipleship." He thought long and hard about the cost of the Calvary Road. As he understood it, for him, it meant finally resisting Adolf Hitler, for which he was hanged in Flossenburg, Germany, on April 9, 1945, at thirty-nine years of age. He saw clearly the deceptiveness of our flesh and need to fight on every front the fight of faith day by day with exultation and humiliation.

> The flesh resists this daily humiliation, first by a frontal attack, and later by hiding itself under the words of the Spirit (i.e., in the name of "evangelical liberty"). We claim liberty from all legal compulsion, from self-martyrdom and mortification and play this off against the proper evangelical use of discipline and asceticism; we thus excuse our self-indulgence and irregularity in prayer, in meditation and in our bodily life. But the contrast between our behavior and the word of Jesus is all too painfully evident. We forget that discipleship means estrangement from the world, and we forget the real joy and freedom which are the outcome of a devout rule of life.[5]

Joy in God is the strength to walk with Jesus from the wilderness to the cross and into eternal life. But maintaining that joy against its most subtle and innocent rivals is a lifelong struggle. And in that struggle, fasting—the humble, hungry handmaid of faith—is an emissary of grace. She comes to every fast with the same words:

> *Though the fig tree should not blossom,*
> *And there be no fruit on the vines,*
> *Though the yield of the olive should fail,*
> *And the fields produce no food,*
> *Though the flock should be cut off from the fold,*
> *And there be no cattle in the stalls,*
> *Yet I will exult in the LORD,*
> *I will rejoice in the God of my salvation.*
> *—Habakkuk 3:17-18*

And when you fast, do not look dismal,
like the hypocrites for they disfigure their faces
that their fasting may be seen by men.
Truly, I say to you, they have received their reward.
But when you fast, anoint your head and wash your face,
that your fasting may not be seen by men
but by your Father who is in secret,
and your Father who sees in secret will reward you.

—MATTHEW 6:16-18, RSV

He loves Thee too little
who loves anything together with Thee
which he loves not for Thy sake.

—ST. AUGUSTINE
The Confessions[1]

Let us learn from our Lord's instruction about fasting,
the great importance of cheerfulness in our religion.
Those words, "anoint thy head, and wash thy face,"
are full of deep meaning. . . . Are we dissatisfied with
Christ's wages, and Christ's service? Surely not! Then
let us not look as if we were.

—J.C. RYLE
Expository Thoughts on the Gospels[2]

3

FASTING FOR THE
REWARD OF THE FATHER

Jesus' Radical
God-Orientation in Fasting

Carl Lundquist was the president of Bethel College and Seminary for almost thirty years. He died in 1991 from skin cancer. In the last decade of his life he devoted a lot of energy to studying and promoting personal spiritual devotion and the disciplines of the Christian life. He even established what he called the "Evangelical Order of the Burning Heart" and began to send out a periodic letter of inspiration and encouragement. In the September, 1989, letter he told the story of how he first began to take fasting seriously.

> My own serious consideration of fasting as a spiritual discipline began as a result of visiting Dr. Joon Gon Kim in Seoul, Korea. "Is it true," I asked him, "that you spent 40 days in fasting prior to the evangelism crusade in 1980?" "Yes," he responded, "it is true." Dr. Kim was chairman of the crusade expected to bring a million people to Yoido Plaza. But six months before the meeting the police informed him they were revoking their permission for the crusade. Korea at that time was in political turmoil and Seoul was under martial

law. The officers decided they could not take the risk of having so many people together in one place. So Dr. Kim and some associates went to a prayer mountain and there spent 40 days before God in prayer and fasting for the crusade. Then they returned and made their way to the police station. "Oh," said the officer when he saw Dr. Kim, "we have changed our mind and you can have your meeting!"

As I went back to the hotel I reflected that I had never fasted like that. Perhaps I had never desired a work of God with the same intensity. . . . His body is marked by many 40-day fasts during his long spiritual leadership of God's work in Asia. Also, however, I haven't seen the miracles Dr. Kim has.

Dr. Lundquist told about one of the "Burning Heart" retreats that he was leading when he saw a seminary senior not eating. He asked him if he was all right and learned that the student was near the end of a twenty-one-day fast as part of seeking God's leading for the next chapter of his life.

Dr. Lundquist said that in the later years of his ministry he found a modified fast very helpful in his life and work. He said,

Instead of taking an hour for lunch I use the time to go to a prayer room, usually the Flame Room in nearby Bethel Theological Seminary. There I spend my lunch break in fellowship with God and in prayer. And I have learned a very personal dimension to what Jesus declared, "I have had meat to eat ye know not of."

I take this to mean that forfeiting food through fasting proved to be a great profit for Dr. Lundquist. In giving up his midday meal to meet with God another way, he found meat to eat in the fellowship of Jesus. "I have meat to eat that ye know not of" (John 4:32 KJV). It seemed that in the Flame Room Carl Lundquist experienced personally the fulfillment of Revelation

3:20, "Behold, I stand at the door and knock; if anyone hears My voice and opens the door, I will come in to him, and will dine with him, and he with Me." In forfeiting physical food Dr. Lundquist found another kind of feast in fellowship with Jesus. He went into his closet away from presidential praise, and the Father rewarded him.

Not If, but When You Fast

One of the texts that moved Dr. Lundquist in those latter years of his life was the one we look at in this chapter, Matthew 6:16-18.

> Whenever you fast, do not put on a gloomy face as the hypocrites do, for they neglect their appearance in order to be seen fasting by men. Truly I say to you, they have their reward in full. But you, when you fast, anoint your head, and wash your face so that you may not be seen fasting by men, but by your Father who is in secret; and your Father who sees in secret will repay you.

The thing that gripped him from this text were the words in verse 16, "Whenever you fast . . ." Like so many others, Dr. Lundquist noticed that it does not say, "*If* you fast," but rather, "*when* you fast." He concluded, as I do, and as most commentators do, that "Jesus takes it for granted that his disciples will observe the pious custom of fasting."[3] Jesus assumed that fasting was a good thing and that it would be done by his disciples. This is what we saw in Chapter One. It's what Jesus underlined when he said in Matthew 9:15, "The days will come when the bridegroom is taken away from them, and then *they will fast*." So in Matthew 6:16-18 Jesus is not teaching on whether we should fast or not. He is assuming we will fast and teaching us how to do it and, especially, how *not* to do it.

How Not to Fast

If Christian fasting should become a part of our lives, as a way of seeking "all the fullness of God" (Ephesians 3:19), then we need to know how not to do it. This does not mean mainly being aware of physical tips on how to avoid headaches, but rather being aware of spiritual dangers that haunt the space of every holy act. The Bible has virtually nothing to say about the physical dangers of fasting. It leaves that secondary matter to our inspection and discretion. But great are the biblical concerns for the spiritual dangers of this sacred deed.

Jesus warns us in Matthew 6:16 not to be like the hypocrites: "Whenever you fast, do not put on a gloomy face as the hypocrites do, for they neglect their appearance in order to be seen fasting by men." So the hypocrites are folks who do their spiritual disciplines "to be seen . . . by men." This is the reward the hypocrites desire. And who has not felt how rewarding indeed it is to be admired for our discipline, or our zeal, or our devotion? This is a great reward among men. Few things feel more gratifying to the heart of fallen man than being made much of for our accomplishments, especially our moral and religious accomplishments.

This craving had infected the religious leaders of Jesus' day in great measure. Concerning the scribes and Pharisees, Jesus warned the people that they "like to walk around in long robes, and like respectful greetings in the market places, and chief seats in the synagogues, and places of honor at banquets, [and that they] devour widows' houses, and for appearance's sake offer long prayers" (Mark 12:38-40). Oh, how strong is the love of the praise of men! We will dress for it ("long robes"), and strut our status in the marketplace for it, and posture ourselves for it at parties, and take up an important pose at church, and even lengthen our prayers to cover our heartless love of money with religious camouflage. All of this we are prone to do because of our seemingly insatiable appetite for the praise of men. We want to be made much of. We want people to like us and admire us and speak well of us. It is a deadly drive. Jesus warned us, "Whoever exalts himself shall be humbled; and whoever humbles himself shall be exalted" (Matthew 23:12).

In Matthew 6:16, Jesus says that if this reward from other people is what you love, this is what you will get. "Truly I say to you, they have their reward in full." In other words, if the reward you aim at in fasting is the admiration of others, that is what you will get, and that will be all you get. In other words, the danger of hypocrisy is that it is so successful. It aims at the praise of men. And it succeeds. But that's all.

Why Is It Hypocrisy for People to Know What You Are Doing?

But there is a problem here. Why is this hypocrisy? Here you have religious people. They decide to fast. Instead of concealing that they are fasting, they make it plain that they are fasting. Why is that hypocrisy? It would seem to be the opposite of hypocrisy. Why isn't it hypocrisy to fast, but to anoint your hair and wash your face and not let anybody know that you are fasting? Isn't the definition of hypocrisy: trying to look different on the outside than you are on the inside? So these religious folks are letting reality show, right? Why are they not the opposite of hypocrites? They fast, and they look like they fast. No sham. Be real. If you fast, look like it.

But Jesus calls them hypocrites. Why? Because the heart that motivates fasting is supposed to be a heart for God. Fasting, in Jesus' way of seeing things, is a hunger for God, or it is worse than nothing. But the heart that motivates their fasting is a hunger for human admiration. So they are being open and transparent about what they are doing, yes, but that very openness is deceptive about what's in their heart. If they wanted to be really open, they would have to wear a sign about their necks that said, "The bottom-line reward in my fasting is the praise of men." Then they would not be hypocrites. They would be openly, transparently, unhypocritically vain. But as it is, they hide their vanity and cloak it with fasting. This is their hypocrisy.

So there are two dangers that these fasting folks have fallen into. *One* is that they are seeking the wrong reward in fasting, namely, the esteem of other people. They love the praise of men. And *the other* is that they hide this with a pretense of love for God. Fasting means love for God—hunger for God. So with their actions they are saying that they have a heart for God. But on the inside they are desperate to be admired and approved by other people.

How Then Shall We Fast?

In Matthew 6:17-18, Jesus gives an alternative to this way of fasting—he describes the way he wants it to be done. He says, "But you, when you fast, anoint your head, and wash your face, so that you may not be seen fasting by men, but by your Father who is in secret; and your Father who sees in secret will repay you."

Does Corporate Fasting Contradict the Word of Jesus?

Now there are all kinds of *public* fasting in the Bible, including the New Testament. For example, in Acts 13:1-3 and 14:23, Paul and Barnabas fast in a way that could not be kept secret. Were they disobedient to Jesus' commandment here? Does Jesus mean that the only fasting that is permitted is private fasting that nobody else can know about? Practically this would almost put fasting out of existence, since even private fasting is nearly impossible to keep secret if one is married or ordinarily takes meals with others.

But there are several contextual reasons for thinking that Jesus was not excluding corporate fasting. One is that the earliest church, including the apostles, practiced public fasting (for example, Acts 13:3). Another is that this section of Matthew 6:1-18 begins with the warning "Beware of practicing your righteousness before men *to be noticed by them*." The point of the whole section is not that public righteousness "before men" is bad, but that doing it "to be noticed by them" is bad. This is confirmed by the fact that even though he said, "When you pray, go into your inner room, and when you have shut your door, pray to your Father who is in secret," nevertheless he himself practiced public prayer (Luke 3:21; 11:1; John 11:41). The motive for praying and fasting is what matters, not whether the acts are public or private.

Another confirmation that not all public fasting is wrong and that what matters is the motive is the fact that Jesus said in Matthew 5:16, "Let your light shine before men in such a way *that they may see your good works*, and glorify your Father who is in heaven." Here he goes beyond saying there are some kinds of righteousness that are public and cannot be concealed (like the ministry of the good Samaritan), but rather he says that the disciples should *want the world to see* this practice of righteousness so that God would be glorified. "Let your light shine before men in such a way *that they may see your good works*." So the motive at stake is not simply whether you want your acts to be known by others, but *why* you want them to be known—that God be glorified, or that you be admired.

I conclude, therefore, that if someone finds out you are fasting, you have not necessarily sinned. The value of your fast is not destroyed if someone notices that you have skipped lunch. It is possible to fast with other people—say, our church pastoral staff fasting on a planning retreat to seek the Lord together—and yet, in that corporate fasting, *not do it* "to be seen by men." Being seen fasting and fasting to be seen are not the same. Being seen fasting is a mere external event. Fasting *to be seen by men*, as Jesus means it here, is a self-exalting motive of the heart.

As usual Jesus is testing our hearts, not just regulating our behavior. He says that when we are fasting, we should not have a heart that wants men to take notice of this discipline and admire us. In fact, he goes beyond this and says that we should make some efforts in the other direction, namely, *not* to be seen fasting. Fix your hair and wash your face so that, as far as possible, people will not even know that you are fasting.

Fasting to Be Seen by the Father

Then he adds the positive counterpart: do all this "so that [you may be seen] by your Father who is in secret." In other words, fast to be seen by God. Fast with a clear intention of being seen by God. As Jesus teaches it, fasting is an intensely Godward act. Do it toward God, who sees when others don't.

Jesus is testing the reality of God in our lives. Do we really have a hunger for God himself, or a hunger for human admiration? O, how easy it is to do religious things if other people are watching! Preaching, praying, attending church, reading the Bible, acts of kindness and charity—they all take on a certain pleasantness of the ego if we know that others will find out about them and think well of us. It is a deadly addiction for esteem that we have.

The Horrible Horizontalizing of Holy Things

But that is not the only defect in the motive of wanting others to see. There is something that assaults God even more directly. It is the subtle sense that grows in us, usually unconsciously, that the real effectiveness of our spiritual acts is at the horizontal level among people, not before the face of God. In other words, if my children see me pray at meals, it will do them good. If the staff sees me fasting, they may be inspired to fast. If my roommate sees me read my Bible, he may be inspired to read his. And so on.

Now that's not all bad. Jesus' public prayers certainly inspired the disciples (Luke 11:1). But the danger is that all of our life—including our spiritual life—starts to be justified and understood simply on the horizontal level for the effects it can have because others see it happening. And so God subtly and slowly can become a secondary Person in the living of our lives. We may think that he is important to us because all these things that we are doing are the kinds of things he wants us to do. But, in fact, he himself is falling out of the picture as the focus of it all. And this registers in the motives of our hearts so that we feel satisfied when others are watching, but feel unmotivated if no one knows what we are doing—no one but God!

What Jesus is doing with these words in Matthew 6 is testing our hearts to see if God himself is our treasure. He is pressing fasting from the external to the radically internal, and making it a sign of our true Godwardness. "To Judaism, a fast was an *outward* sign of an inward condition. To Jesus, a fast was an *inward* sign of an inward condition."[4] He is testing to see if the admiration of other people or even the spiritual effect on others of our piety has become the God-supplanting food that entices our soul. How do we feel when nobody else knows what we are doing? How is it when no one is saying, "How goes the fast?" Are we content in God when no one but God knows that we have done what we ought to have done?

Jesus is calling for a radical orientation on God himself. He is pushing us to have a real, utterly authentic, personal relationship with God. If God is not real to us—personally, vitally real to us—it will be miserable to endure something difficult with God alone as the one who knows. It will all seem very pointless, because the whole range of horizontal possibilities will be nullified since no one knows what we are going through. All that matters is God, and who he is, and what he thinks, and what he will do.

What Reward Should We Seek in Our Fasting?

Which brings us to the last part of verse 18 and the promise Jesus makes about what God will do for those who focus vertically on him and do not need the praise of men to make their devotion worthwhile. He says, "And your Father who sees in secret will repay you." It is good and right to want and to seek the reward of God in fasting. Jesus would not have offered this to us if it were defective to reach for it. I have argued for decades that seeking the reward of the Father is not sub-Christian or unloving or contrary to true virtue.[5] As C.S. Lewis said:

> There are rewards that do not sully motives. A man's love for a woman is not mercenary because he wants to marry her, nor his love for poetry mercenary because he wants to read it, nor his love for exercise less interested because he wants to run and leap and walk. Love, by definition, seeks to enjoy its object.[6]

Doing right "just because it is right" is not the Christian ideal. Doing right to enlarge our delight in God is. So here again the question arises: shall we hear Jesus and learn, or shall we bring our philosophy from outside the Bible and silence him again?

Jesus says, "[Fast not to be seen by men but] by your Father who is in secret; and your Father who sees in secret will repay you." The English word "repay" (NASB) is probably a misleading translation because of the mercenary connotations of the word. It seems to suggest that fasting is a kind of performance we render for God that then obliges him to pay us wages or some honorarium. But the Greek word *(apodōsei)* does not carry that necessary connotation. It may refer to paying back financial debts (for example, Matthew 5:26), but not always. It was the word used for Pilate's giving the body of Jesus to Joseph of Arimathea (Matthew 27:58), and Jesus' handing the scroll back to the synagogue leader after reading it (Luke 4:20), and Jesus' returning the healed boy to his father (Luke 9:42), and the apostle's giving witness to the resurrection (Acts 4:33), and God's giving Paul a crown of righteousness (1 Timothy 4:8). The word itself does not imply a business transaction of work and wages.

How then should we think about God's rewarding those who fast not for the praise of men, but to be seen by God? God sees us fasting. He sees that we have a deep longing that is pulling us away from the ordinary good uses of the world in order to fast. He sees that our hearts are not seeking the common pleasures of human admiration and applause. He sees that we are acting not out of strength to impress others with our discipline, or even out of a desire to influence others to imitate our devotion. But we have come to God out of weakness to express to him our need and our great longing that he would manifest himself more fully in our lives for the joy of our soul and the glory of his name.

How to Make a Cuckold out of God by Fasting

And when God sees this, he responds. He acts. He rewards. What is the "repayment" or the "reward" that Jesus promises from the Father in these verses? In a perverse way, one might even wonder if the reward God promises is "the praise of men"—as if God said, Since you did not seek it by public fasting but looked to me,

I will give you this longed-for wish of human praise. If we hoped for this, our fasting would make a cuckold out of God.

This is what James 4:3-4 makes clear. James pictures prayer as a petition to our heavenly husband. Then he ponders the possibility that we would actually ask our husband to pay for our visit to the prostitute. "You ask and do not receive, because you ask with wrong motives, so that you may spend it on your pleasures. You adulteresses, do you not know that friendship with the world is hostility toward God?" The word "adulteresses" is the key here. Why are we called "adulteresses" in praying for something to spend on our pleasures? Because God is our husband and the "world" is a prostitute luring us to give affections to her that belong only to God. This is how subtle the sin of worldliness can be. It can emerge not against prayer, but in prayer—and fasting. We begin to pray and fast—even intensely—not for God as our all-satisfying husband, but only for his gifts in the world so that we can make love with them.

No, the reward we are to seek from the Father in fasting is not first or mainly the gifts of God, but God himself. Where in the context might we look for the reward that the Father encourages us to seek? I think a reliable guide would be the prayer that Jesus just taught us to pray in Matthew 6:9-13. It begins with three main longings that we are to hope for from God. First, that God's name be hallowed or revered; second, that God's kingdom come; and third, that his will be done on earth the way it's done in heaven. That is the first and primary reward Jesus tells us to seek in our praying and our fasting. We fast out of longing for God's name to be known and cherished and honored, and out of longing for his kingly rule to be extended and then consummated in history, and out of longing for his will to be done everywhere with the same devotion and energy that the indefatigable angels do it sleeplessly in heaven forever and ever.

Wanting What Is Not God for God's Sake

To be sure, God gives us our daily bread—and many other things through prayer and fasting. And it is not wrong to seek specifically for his help in every area of our lives. But these three petitions—that his name be hallowed, that his kingdom come, and that his will be done—test and prove whether all the other things we long for are expressions of our hunger for God, or whether his gifts are vying for his own place of supremacy and preciousness in our lives. The supremacy of God in all things is the great reward we long for in fasting. His supremacy in our own affections and in all our life-choices. His supremacy in the purity of the church. His supremacy in the salvation of the lost. His supremacy in the establishing of righteousness and justice. And his supremacy for the joy of all peoples in the evangelization of the world.

Seeking from God the reward of God's all-satisfying supremacy puts all other desires to the test. Are they for God's sake? This is the ultimate reason why Jesus called us to fast without wanting to be seen by others. Not just so that we could get worldly desires satisfied from God rather than men (and thus make God party to our spiritual adultery), but so that we would count God himself as our desire, and all else a subordinate spin-off of his enthralling glory.

And so we ask, as we fast and pray, Do we want to conquer bad habits and old enslavements, to remove every obstacle to the fullest enjoyment of God, so that people might see and give him glory? Do we want our prodigal sons and wayward daughters to come home because this would honor God's name? Do we want our churches to grow because the hallowing of Christ's name is at stake among unbelievers? Do we want China and North Korea and Saudi Arabia and Iraq and Libya to open their doors to the gospel for the sake of the advance of the kingship of Jesus? Do we want upright leaders in government because this world is meant to magnify the goodness and justice of God?

This is what Jesus is calling us to—a radically God-oriented living and praying and fasting. So for the sake of your own soul, and in response to Jesus, and for the advancement of God's supremacy in all things for the joy of all peoples, comb your hair, and wash your face, and let the Father who sees in secret observe how hungry you are for him with fasting. The Father who sees in secret is brimming with rewards for your joy and for his glory.

Anna . . . never left the temple,
serving night and day with fastings and prayers.
. . . She began giving thanks to God,
and continued to speak of him to all those
who were looking for the redemption of Jerusalem.

—LUKE 2:36-38

In the future there is laid up for me
the crown of righteousness,
which the Lord, the righteous Judge,
will award to me on that day;
and not only to me, but also to all
who have loved His appearing.
. . . Amen. Come, Lord Jesus!

—2 TIMOTHY 4:8; REVELATION 22:20

Do you love the Lord's appearing? Then you will bend every effort to take the gospel into all the world. It troubles me in the light of the clear teaching of God's Word, in the light of our Lord's explicit definition of our task in The Great Commission, that we take it so lightly. . . . His is the kingdom; He reigns in heaven, and He manifests His reign on earth in and through His church. When we have accomplished our mission, He will return and establish His kingdom in glory. To us it is given not only to wait for but also to hasten the coming of the day of God.

—GEORGE LADD
The Gospel of the Kingdom[1]

4

FASTING FOR THE
KING'S COMING

How Much
Do We Miss Him?

Fasting is a physical expression of heart-hunger for the coming of Jesus. We have seen in Matthew 9:15 (Chapter One) that Jesus pictured himself as the Bridegroom of the Church. He explained that his disciples were not fasting because the Bridegroom is present. But then he said, "The days will come when the Bridegroom is taken away from them, and they will fast." So Jesus connects Christian fasting with our longing for the return of the Bridegroom. Therefore, one of the most important meanings of Christian fasting is to express the hunger of our hearts for the coming of our King.

Fasting and the Lord's Supper

Fasting is a future-oriented counterpart to the past-oriented celebration of the Lord's Supper. Jesus said, "Do this in remembrance of me" (Luke 22:19). By eating we remember the past and say, Jesus has come. He has died for our sins. He has risen from the dead. Our guilt is removed. Our sin is forgiven. Our condemnation and punishment have been transferred to Christ. Our acquittal is sealed. Our reconciliation with God is accomplished. Our bondage to sin is broken. Our enemy has been put to naught. The sting of death is removed. The destiny of hell is averted. Eternal life has been given. The Lord has come! Let us feast on these great realities and establish our souls on the great foundation of God's grace in the death and resurrection of Christ.

That is what we say in our eating of the Lord's Supper. But by not eating—by fasting—we look to the future with an aching in our hearts saying: "Yes, he came. And yes, what he did for us is glorious. But precisely because of what we have seen and what we have tasted, we feel keenly his absence as well as his presence. The Bridegroom has gone away. He is not here. He was here, and he loved us to the uttermost. And we can eat and even celebrate with feasting because he has come. But this we also know: he is not here the way he once was. As Paul said, "While we are at home in the body we are *absent from the Lord.*" And his absence is painful. The sin and misery of the world is painful. The people of Christ are weak and despised—like sheep in the midst of wolves (Matthew 10:16). We long for him to come again and take up his throne and reign in our midst and vindicate his people and his truth and his glory.

I do not mean to claim that the Lord instituted fasting with the same formality and finality that he instituted the Lord's Supper. Never did he say concerning fasting, "Do this until I come." Nevertheless, he did say, "The days will come when the Bridegroom is taken away from them, and they will fast." It is not a command or an instituted ordinance. But it is a prediction. It is a statement of what will seem normal for those who love the Bridegroom and miss him.

Crying for Him Day and Night

Fasting poses the question: do we miss him? How hungry are we for him to come? The almost universal absence of regular fasting for the Lord's return is a witness to our satisfaction with the presence of the world and the absence of the Lord. This is not the way it should be. In Luke 18:7-8 Jesus says,

> *"Shall not God bring about justice for His elect, who cry to Him day and night, and will He delay long over them? I tell you that He will bring about justice for them speedily. However, when the Son of Man comes, will He find faith on the earth?"*

The point of these verses is that the Son of Man is coming again. When he comes, he will bring about justice for his elect. They will no longer appear as "the scum of the world, the dregs of all things" (1 Corinthians 4:13), but will "shine forth as the sun in the kingdom of their Father" (Matthew 13:43). While the faith of many will fail and the love of many will grow cold (Matthew 24:12), the Son of Man, when he comes, will find his elect persevering with faith and love to the end (Mark 13:13).

But notice the condition of these elect who are vindicated when he comes. Jesus says that they "cry to him day and night." This is what is missing in the comfortable Christian Church of the modern world. Where in the West do Christians cry to Christ day and night that he would come and bring about justice for his elect? Where is there that kind of longing and aching for the consummation of the kingdom? It is no surprise then, that the question of *fasting* for the coming of the Bridegroom is scarcely asked. If the cry itself is not there, why would one even think of expressing it with fasting?

Come, Lord Jesus!

What is the cry? What was the cry of the early church? The cry of the early church was, "Come, Lord Jesus!" It is no mere coincidence that the very last words of the Bible are first the words of the Lord, "Yes, I am coming quickly," and then the response of the church: "Amen. Come, Lord Jesus" (Revelation 22:20). This is the cry that the whole Bible is meant to leave in the hearts of the elect.

One of the few Aramaic words that the first-century Greek-speaking church preserved from the treasured language of Jesus and his earliest followers was the word *Maranatha*. In 1 Corinthians 16:22 Paul closes his letter by saying, "If anyone does not love the Lord, let him be accursed. *Maranatha*." The word means, "Our Lord, come!" There is little doubt that the word was preserved in its original Aramaic for the same reason "Amen" has been preserved, in its Hebrew form without change, in almost every language of the world: it was a constantly used form. "*Maranatha*" was the ever-present heart-cry of the early church. "O Lord, come!"

Jesus had taught his disciples to pray, "Thy kingdom come" (Matthew 6:10). And he had taught them that the kingdom would come in its fullness when he himself comes again "in the glory of His Father with His angels" (Matthew 16:27). Therefore the prayer, "Thy kingdom come," was virtually identical with the prayer, "*Maranatha*!" "Come, Lord Jesus!" We can see how central this heart-cry was to the early church. These are not peripheral concerns. They are central to the whole ethos of the body of Christ. The Bridegroom left on a journey just before the wedding, and the Bride cannot act as if things are normal. If she loves him, she will ache for his return.

Do We Love the Appearing of the Lord?

In fact Paul speaks of *loving* the appearing of the Lord and makes it a test of authentic faith. He says, at the end of his life, "In the future there is laid up for me the crown of righteousness, which the Lord, the righteous Judge, will award to me on that day; and

not only to me, but also to all who have *loved His appearing*"
(2 Timothy 4:8). The crown of righteousness is not a reward for
only some that divides the elect into righteous and unrighteous.
It is the crown that all God's people receive. It is the "crown of
life which the Lord has promised to those who love Him" (James
1:12) and are faithful unto death (Revelation 2:10). Therefore,
loving the appearing of the Lord is not an optional Christian act
that may earn more rewards. It is what true Christian faith does:
it loves Christ and longs for the Bridegroom to come. Saving faith
says, "Thy kingdom come! Come back, O precious Bridegroom.
Come, reign as King. Come, vindicate your people. Come, marry
your bride."

What Anna Teaches Us About Longing

In foreseeing that the Bride would fast for the coming of the
Bridegroom (Matthew 15:9), Jesus was not imagining something
unheard of. The precedent for fasting for the kingdom of God
was known among the saints of his day. Luke gives us a glimpse
of it in Luke 2:36-38.

> *And there was a prophetess, Anna the daughter of Phanuel,*
> *of the tribe of Asher. She was advanced in years, having lived*
> *with a husband seven years after her marriage, and then as*
> *a widow to the age of eighty-four. And she never left the tem-*
> *ple,* serving night and day with fastings and prayers. *And at*
> *that very moment she came up and began giving thanks to*
> *God, and continued to speak of Him to all those who were*
> *looking for the redemption of Jerusalem.*

Mary and Joseph had just brought the infant Jesus into the
temple. Luke tells us about two very old people—Simeon and
Anna—who recognize who he is. What marks both of these people is that they were yearning and longing for the coming of the

Messiah. In verse 25 Luke says that Simeon was "looking for the consolation of Israel, and the Holy Spirit was on him."

In verse 37 he tells us that Anna virtually never left the temple and was serving the Lord "with fastings and prayers." In other words, she was just like Simeon—she was longing for the Messiah to come; she was fasting and praying night and day because she was looking for the redemption of Jerusalem.

In verse 38 she comes at just the right moment to see the Messiah-child, and she gives thanks to God and speaks of him to all who were "looking for the redemption of Jerusalem." In other words, God gave a special glimpse of the King's glory to those who were yearning and longing and looking for "the redemption of Jerusalem." For Anna that yearning meant a life of *fasting* and praying, decade after decade—probably sixty years since her husband died—as she ministered in the temple.

I think Luke tells us about Simeon and Anna to illustrate the way holy and devout people feel about the promise of Christ's coming, and how God responds to their longings. They see more than others see. They may not understand fully all the details about how the Messiah is coming—Simeon and Anna surely didn't—but God mercifully gives them, before they die, a glimpse of what they so passionately wanted to see.

Shall We Long for Him Less?

Now here we are on the other side of the King's coming. He has come and gone away again. He has revealed his glory. He has shed his blood for our sins. He has risen from the dead. He has ascended into heaven to sit at the Father's right hand until he puts all his enemies under his feet. He has sent his Holy Spirit to regenerate us and sanctify us and indwell us. He has commissioned his church to disciple the nations. And he has promised in John 14:3, "I will come again."

How does our situation compare to Anna's? Her hopes were based on the promises of God like ours are. But oh, how much more we have seen than she had seen. How much more of the Messiah we know and can hope for! She had never seen the years of compassion and power as we have. She had never heard the words of authority and wisdom and love as we have. She never saw the blind receive their sight and the lame walk and the lepers cleansed and the deaf hear and the dead raised and the poor evangelized the way Jesus did it. She never saw him consecrate himself in Gethsemane, or be crucified for our sakes on Golgotha. She never heard the merciful words, "Today you will be with me in Paradise," or the triumphant words, "It is finished." She never saw him risen from the dead triumphant over sin and death and hell. And yet from what she knew of him in the Old Testament, she yearned for him and fasted with prayers night and day awaiting "the redemption of Israel."

But we have seen all these things. We know the Savior a hundred times better than Anna did. And now this one, whom we know so well, is gone. We walk by faith and not by sight. The Bridegroom whom we love was taken away. The wedding party was broken up. It is as though the wedding march had started and we were walking down the aisle to him, and at the last minute he disappeared.

Shall we long for him less than Anna longed for him? Does the fact that we have watched him live and love for three years and even now have his Spirit—does this make us feel Anna's longing less or more? Oh, what an indictment of our blindness or our dullness if the answer is: less.

Fasting's Freedom from the Sensualizing of the Soul

One of the great effects of fasting is that it assists what it expresses. I mean that fasting is mainly an expression of the soul's hunger for God. It is not a contrived means to make us love God. We love him and long for him. And then fasting rises up as a way of saying earnestly with our whole body what our hearts feel: I hunger for you, O God. Fasting expresses, rather than creates, hunger for God.

Nevertheless, it is also true that the very nature of fasting makes it an assistant to this hunger for God. The reason is that hunger for God is spiritual, not physical. And we are less sensitive to spiritual appetites when we are in the bondage of physical ones. This means that fasting is a way of awakening us to latent spiritual appetites by pushing the domination of physical forces from the center of our lives. John Wesley expressed this as well as anyone I have read. What he calls the "sensualizing" of the soul is a great hindrance to our longing for Jesus to return. Therefore fasting assists the very experience of hunger for God that it also expresses.

Fullness of bread [increases] not only carelessness and levity of spirit, but also foolish and unholy desires, yea, unclean and vile affections. . . . Even a genteel, regular sensuality is continually sensualizing the soul, and sinking it into a level with the beasts that perish. It cannot be expressed what an effect a variety and delicacy of food have on the mind as well as the body; making it just ripe for every pleasure of sense, as soon as opportunity shall invite. Therefore, on this ground also, every wise man will refrain his soul, and keep it low; will wean it more and more from all those indulgences of the inferior appetites, which naturally tend to chain it down to earth, and to pollute as well as debase it. Here is another perpetual reason for fasting; to remove the food of lust and sensuality, to withdraw the incentives of foolish and hurtful desires, of vile and vain affections.[2]

I do not mean to belittle the good gifts of God, as if eating were an evil or even a hindrance to spiritual sensitivity. Together with Wesley I simply mean to say that most of us run the risk of being overly "sensualized" simply by having every craving satisfied and rarely pausing in a moment of self-denial to discover if there are alive within us spiritual appetites that could satisfy us at a much deeper level than food, and that are designed for the honor of God. Such is the appetite for the coming of King Jesus.

The Master Comes to Serve!

Consider how the New Testament describes the hearts of believers as they lived in the shadow of the Lord's coming. They recalled the words of the Lord Jesus, from one of his most stunning parables: "Be like men who are waiting for their master when he returns from the wedding feast, so that they may immediately open the door to him when he comes and knocks" (Luke 12:35). I refer to this as a stunning parable because it portrays the returning Christ as a "master" who nevertheless "will gird himself to serve, and have them [his servants] recline at the table, and will come up and wait on them" (Luke 12:37). This takes the breath away. The one we wait for, who will come in the clouds with the holy angels and the glory of his Father and terrify the nations—this one will magnify his greatness in mercy and servanthood and make himself the servant of our joy forever. Not even after the second coming will he be "served by human hands, as though He needed anything, since He Himself gives to all life and breath and all things" (Acts 17:25).

So the early Christians recalled the words of Jesus that we are to "be like men who are waiting for their master"—and such a Servant-master as this! It is a different image than the Bridegroom, but no less evocative of joy. So they believed that the second coming of Jesus, no matter what suffering they had to go through, would be an all-recompensing experience of joy and exultation. "To the degree that you share the sufferings of Christ, keep on rejoicing; so that also at the revelation of His glory, you may rejoice with exultation" (1 Peter 4:13).

The Passions of an Exile

This hope was so dominant for the early Christians that all of life was lived as the life of an exile. This did not mean that they had no concern for the welfare of their neighbors. On the contrary, it was the lavish freedom from the love of things that gave them the liberty to love their neighbors with abandon. And this freedom came from their otherworldly hope. The sacrificial love of believers for their neighbors was the evidence that their hope came from outside this world order (Colossians 1:4-5; Hebrews 10:32-34). Their common confession was, "here we have no lasting city" (Hebrews 13:14). We are "aliens and strangers" (1 Peter 2:11). And this meant that the great, joyful, love-sustaining expectation was the coming of their king: "Our citizenship is in heaven, from which also we eagerly wait for a Savior, the Lord Jesus Christ" (Philippians 3:20).

This "eager expectation" pervades the New Testament and defines what it means to belong to Christ. "Christ, having been offered once to bear the sins of many, will appear a second time, not to deal with sin but to save those who are *eagerly waiting for him*" (Hebrews 9:28, RSV). "You are not lacking in any gift, *awaiting eagerly the revelation of our Lord Jesus Christ*" (1 Corinthians 1:7). "Deny ungodliness and worldly desires . . . *looking [eagerly] for the blessed hope* and the appearing of the glory of our great God and Savior, Christ Jesus" (Titus 2:13). "Keep yourselves in the love of God, *waiting anxiously for the mercy of our Lord Jesus Christ* to eternal life" (Jude 21).

This "eager waiting" of the early church for her

Bridegroom to come explains why she prayed the way she did. You can't really long for something as intensely as she longed for Christ and not cry out to God. So she cried out and prayed, "Lord, thy kingdom come!" "*Maranatha*!" "Come, Lord Jesus!" Surely, this hunger for Christ needs to be restored in the comfortable church of the prosperous West. The absence of fasting is indicative of our comfort with the way things are. No one fasts to express how content they are. People only fast out of dissatisfaction. "The attendants of the bridegroom cannot mourn as long as the bridegroom is with them, can they? But the days will come when the bridegroom is taken away from them, and then they will fast" (Matthew 15:9). The absence of fasting is the measure of our contentment with the absence of Christ.

Fasting for the King Is Not a Pacifistic Discipline

But it would be a great mistake to think that the awakening of desire for the Bridegroom would produce a wave of monastic withdrawal into the fasting and prayer of passive waiting. That is not what the awakening of desire for Christ would produce. It would produce a radical, new commitment to complete the task of world evangelization, no matter what the cost. And fasting would not become a pacifistic discipline for private hopes, but a fearsome missionary weapon in the fight of faith.

The reason I say this is simple. If we really long for Christ to return and the kingdom to come, then we will pour our lives into completing the prerequisite to his coming, namely, Matthew 24:14—"This gospel of the kingdom shall be preached in the whole world for a witness to all the nations, and then the end shall come." The end will not come until every nation (= every people group)[3] receives a credible testimony to the gospel of Christ. "We must humbly admit that only God will know when this sign will have been completely fulfilled."[4] That it will be fulfilled rests on him who said, "Heaven and earth will pass away, but My words shall not pass away" (Matthew 24:35).

He Will Not Come Before the Work Is Done

George Ladd was one of my professors in seminary, and it amazed me that few things stirred him more deeply than the failure of the church to see the connection between world evangelization and the return of the Lord.

> God alone, who has told us that this Gospel of the kingdom shall be preached in the whole world for a testimony unto all the nations, will know when that objective has been accomplished. But I do not need to know. I know only one thing: Christ has not yet returned; therefore, the task is not yet done. When it is done, Christ will come. Our responsibility is not to insist on defining the terms of our task; our responsibility is to complete it. So long as Christ does not return, our work is not done. Let us get busy and complete our mission. . . . Do you love the Lord's appearing? Then you will bend every effort to take the gospel into all the world. It troubles me, in the light of the clear teaching of God's Word, in the light of our Lord's explicit definition of our task in The Great Commission (Matthew 28:18-20), that we take it so lightly. . . . His is the kingdom; He reigns in heaven and He manifests His reign on earth in and through His church. When we have accomplished our mission, He will return and establish His kingdom in glory. To us it is given not only to wait for, but also to hasten the coming of the day of God (2 Peter 3:12).[5]

In other words, there is a direct correlation between loving the Lord's appearing and laboring for the cause of world evangelization. This simply deepens the connection between fasting and the coming of Christ. We will see in Chapter Five how fasting has turned the course of world history precisely in unleashing the first great missionary thrust in Acts 13:1-4. This fits with Jesus' words that his disciples will fast out of longing for the Bridegroom. For the Bridegroom will not come until the gospel is preached to the nations, and the nations are reached through spiritual breakthroughs that come by fasting and prayer.

Prayer and Preaching, Intensified by Fasting

So there are at least these two ways that the Church—the Bride— is to express her longing for the Bridegroom: first by prayer ("Thy kingdom come . . . *Maranatha* . . . Come, Lord Jesus!") and second by world evangelization ("This gospel will be preached to all the nations . . . then the end [the Lord!] will come"). And since Jesus said, "when the Bridegroom is taken away, [we] will fast," it is not surprising that fasting is connected with precisely these two things in the New Testament: prayer (Luke 2:37; Matthew 6:6-18) and world evangelization (Acts 13:1-4). Fasting is the exclamation point at the end of "*Maranatha*, come, Lord Jesus!" It is the modest, voluntary embracing of what it will cost to finish the Great Commission: pain. By it we go—or join with those who go—and say, "O, make me a means of your conquering the nations and your coming again!"

Let us long for him and look for him with more intensity than Anna and Simeon. Shall we have less devotion than these pre-Christian saints? We have beheld his glory. Glory as of the only begotten of the Father. And shall we hunger less for his appearing? Are we settled into the world so comfortably that the thought of fasting for the end of history is unthinkable?

Let Us Do It for the King!

What about you older people? Can you taste the glories of the presence of the King better because they are nearer? Do you turn that taste into fasting for the King's coming? What about you younger people? Do you love Jesus so much that his coming would be the greatest thing you can imagine? Or is he a kind of weekend topic of religious talk that sometimes helps you with a bad conscience, but isn't someone you would want to interrupt your life? What about the middle-aged among us? How do you feel about being told that fasting for the King's coming may reflect how much you want the Bridegroom to come? Do your plans for that long-awaited retirement fill you with stronger desires than does the prospect of Christ's coming? Does Anna's passion for the Messiah appeal to any of us at all? Do we want the appearance of Jesus more than we want to finish our career and family plans? Or our next meal?

Should we not fast for the coming of the king? This is not some strange new devotional practice. It is simply saying with our hunger: This much, O Lord, we want your work to be done and your kingdom to come. This much, O Lord, we want you to return!

Now there were at Antioch,
in the church that was there,
prophets and teachers:
Barnabas, and Simeon who was called Niger,
and Lucius of Cyrene, and Manaen
who had been brought up with Herod the tetrarch, and Saul.
And while they were ministering to the Lord and fasting,
the Holy Spirit said,
"Set apart for Me Barnabas and Saul
for the work to which I have called them."

—ACTS 13:1-3

The state of the times extremely requires a fullness of the divine Spirit in ministers, and we ought to give ourselves no rest till we have obtained it. And in order to [do] this, I should think ministers, above all persons, ought to be much in secret prayer and fasting, and also much in praying and fasting one with another. It seems to me it would be becoming the circumstances of the present day, if ministers in a neighborhood would often meet together and spend days in fasting and fervent prayer among themselves, earnestly seeking for those extraordinary supplies of divine grace from heaven, that we need at this day.

—JONATHAN EDWARDS
Some Thoughts Concerning the Revival[1]

5

FASTING AND THE
COURSE OF HISTORY

A Call for
Discernment and Desire

It is dangerous to hold up a person or ministry or church as a model of fasting. As soon as we do, the clay feet will become plain. Disillusionment often follows naive admiration. There is none without sin, and all our triumphs are mixed with imperfections. We do well to temper our esteem with the acknowledgment that there are hidden faults in every saint, and today's victory is no assurance of tomorrow's holiness. Nor can we even read the heart behind today's triumph. Neither the heart of others nor our own (1 Corinthians 4:4). What's more, the moving stories that we hear about fasting have often passed through many minds and many mouths of fallible folks like us.

Let Your Exultation Be in the Word of God

All of this I say simply to caution us from transferring the root of our exultation from the historic *Word* of God written to the contemporary *work* of God reported. God alone never changes, but the outpourings of his blessings ebb and flow in ways far too mysterious for our small minds to judge. The moment we think righteousness holds sway, some sinful plague is spreading in the midst. And just when we think the darkness is so thick that all is lost, someone grabs a rope that rings a bell and brings an army with torches. We will only maintain our stability and unshakable confidence if we keep our focus on the unchanging God and take every rising or receding tide as a work of infinite wisdom for the accomplishment of God's holy purposes.

Nevertheless, God ordains in his Word that we take heart from those who have known the grace of God before us. "[Do] not be sluggish, but imitators of those who through faith and patience inherit the promises. . . . Remember those who led you, who spoke the word of God to you; and considering the result of their conduct, imitate their faith" (Hebrews 6:12; 13:7). It would signal more pride in us than sin in them if we refused to be inspired and guided by ordinary saints who come into extraordinary blessings. So it is with fasting. The Bible and the history of the Church are strewn with stories of God's remarkable work in gracious response to the fasting and prayer of his people. These stories are not there to be ignored. Nor are they there as a panacea for every lukewarm season in the life of faith. Oh, how hasty we are to judge from God's mercy in the life of a fasting saint that this particular pattern of piety is the key to vital spiritual life!

Finney's Fasting and Imperfections

For example, many have read the story of Charles Finney's (1792-1875) conversion and his subsequent experience of fasting, and have taken it as a normative way of maintaining a revived state.

> To the honor of God alone I will say a little of my own experience in this matter. I was powerfully converted on the

morning of the 10th of October. In the evening of the same day, and on the morning of the following day, I received overwhelming baptisms of the Holy Ghost, that went through me, as it seemed to me, body and soul. I immediately found myself endued with such power from on high that a few words dropped here and there to individuals were the means of their immediate conversion. My words seemed to fasten like barbed arrows in the souls of men. They cut like a sword. They broke the heart like a hammer. Multitudes can attest to this. Oftentimes a word dropped, without my remembering it, would fasten conviction, and often result in almost immediate conversion. Sometimes I would find myself, in a great measure, empty of this power. I would go out and visit, and find that I made no saving impression. I would exhort and pray, with the same result. *I would then set apart a day for private fasting and prayer, fearing that this power had departed from me, and would inquire anxiously after the reason of this apparent emptiness. After humbling myself, and crying out for help, the power would return upon me with all its freshness. This has been the experience of my life.*[2]

What shall we do with a testimony like this? Shall we conclude that repeated days of prayer and fasting are the key to continuous revival? Shall we discount its relevance for us because it was just one man's unique experience with God? Surely somewhere between these two extremes is the humble and sober answer. We are not so wise and experienced in the things of God that we cannot learn from another's fight of faith. God may indeed inspire us to set aside a day of fasting as we read this, and he may meet us there with great reviving power. But he may not. Others have sought and found awakening without fasting. Still others fasted and prayed for two, three, four or more weeks before a breakthrough came. It is a mistake to think that God's way with one of his children will be his way with all.

Another mistake we can make in admiring the work of God in the lives of fasting saints is to think that God's blessing implies his approval of their behavior and doctrine. But this is not necessarily the case. We find it difficult to imagine why God blesses a person's ministry if the doctrine is defective and if resilient sins infect the heart. But God seemed to be using Apollos, for example, who was "mighty in the Scriptures," but to whom Priscilla and Aquila had to "explain the way of God more accurately" (Acts 18:24-26). And Jesus warns that in the judgment some will say, "Did we not prophesy in Your name, and in Your name cast out demons, and in Your name perform many miracles?" But he will say to them, "I never knew you" (Matthew 7:22-23). In other words, the test of truth and righteousness is not whether there is power in a person's ministry.

Charles Finney, for example, held to a theology that was deeply at odds with his Calvinistic contemporary Asahel Nettleton (1812-1844). But both were used by God in evangelism.[3] Similarly John Wesley (the Arminian) and George Whitefield (the Calvinist) were used by God to bring thousands of people into the kingdom of Christ. The inference from this should not be that doctrine is a matter of indifference. The longterm harm of holding false views of God and salvation is not nullified by short-term evidences of God's undeserved blessing. In fact, in the case of Finney, there is good evidence that he himself regretted some of his own spiritual tactics, if not his defective views of God's sovereignty.[4] The remarkable fact is that God has his wise and sovereign purposes for using defective people and defective theology to save sinners. This is not a blessing on error, but a grace in spite of it. The banner over every blessing of God on defective lives and doctrine is Romans 2:4—do you not know that God's kindness and forbearance and patience are meant to lead you to repentance?

Therefore, no experience of fasting is sufficient to win our imitation without other considerations coming into play. We will measure all by the Scriptures. We will not be swept away by the "successes" or "blessings" that accompany any particular pattern of spiritual discipline. We will realize that God is sovereign in dispensing his mercies: "I will be gracious to whom I will be gracious, and will show compassion on whom I will show compassion" (Exodus 33:19). And we will humble ourselves to learn from the experience of others, even those we may disagree with, since God has mercy and gives lessons in unlikely places.

Fasting and the Course of Korean History

With that caution, let us now observe, without fear of being carried away, that the course of history has been changed repeatedly through fasting and prayer. Many examples could be given. In the latter years of the twentieth century, fasting and prayer have almost become synonymous with the churches of South Korea. And there is good reason. The first Protestant church was planted in Korea in 1884. One hundred years later there were 30,000 churches. That's an average of 300 new churches a year for 100 years. At the end of the twentieth century, evangelicals comprise about 30% of the population. God has used many means to do this great work. One of them is a recovery not just of dynamic prayer, but of fasting-prayer. For example, in the OMS (Overseas Missionary Society) churches alone more than 20,000 people have completed a forty-day fast—usually at one of their "prayer houses" in the mountains.[5]

For anyone who has a passion for the supremacy of God, such a story cannot pass without awakening some strong desires. Here at the end of the twentieth century most denominations in America are stagnant, with far less impact on our unbelieving culture than we long for. In Europe, the countries of the once blazing Reformation are now considered "post-Christian" and coldly resistant to life-changing evangelism. How can we not stand up and ask: could it be that the Lord would appoint a new season of fasting and prayer as a way forward in our day?

Fasting and the Epoch-making Word at Antioch

One of the clearest biblical encouragements to consider fasting as a history-shaping act is found in Acts 13:1-4:

> Now there were at Antioch, in the church that was there, prophets and teachers: Barnabas, and Simeon who was called Niger, and Lucius of Cyrene, and Manaen who had been brought up with Herod the tetrarch, and Saul. And while they were ministering to the Lord and fasting, the Holy Spirit said, "Set apart for Me Barnabas and Saul for the work to which I have called them. Then, when they had fasted and prayed and laid their hands on them, they sent them away. So, being sent out by the Holy Spirit, they went down to Seleucia and from there they sailed to Cyprus.

The situation is that Saul (Paul) and Barnabas and some of the other leaders in the church in Antioch were worshiping—"ministering to the Lord"—and fasting (verse 2). Judging by what happened we may assume, I think, that the burden they had as a leadership team in the church was this: "Where do we go from here as a church?" They were fasting to seek the leading of the Holy Spirit in the direction of their mission. The upshot was more magnificent than any master planning effort the church has ever undertaken.

They were hungry enough for God's leading that they wanted to say it with the hunger of their bodies and not just the hunger of their hearts. "We want you and we want your leading, O God! O Holy Spirit, what is your will for the mission of this church? We want to see you and follow you more than we want to eat."

Questions the Bible Does Not Answer

One of the things that boggles my mind about planning efforts in the local church where I have served now for over seventeen years is that many of the questions we need to answer are not answered in the Bible, at least not directly. They are the kind of questions, I think, that the leaders in Antioch were facing: "Lord, shall we begin a world missions program? Should it be now? Should we send some of our own teachers as the first missionaries? Should it be Saul or Simeon or Niger or Lucius or Barnabas? Should we send two or three or four? Which way should we send them: by land or by sea? Should we fund them fully, or expect them to work for their keep, or hope that there will be 'sons of peace' in the towns where they go who will feed them? Should other churches join with us?" Etc., etc.

Most of the questions that church planning teams have to answer are of that kind. Where will we get the answers? I do not minimize the sound and basic teaching of the Bible that we should be "transformed by the renewing of [our] mind, that [we] may prove what the will of God is, that which is good and acceptable and perfect." But this "proving" of the will of God in non-moral matters (should we send Saul and Barnabas or Lucius and Simeon?) is not a mechanical thing. Paul prayed earnestly that believers would "be filled with the knowledge of [God's] will in all *spiritual wisdom* and understanding . . . and bear fruit in every good work" (Colossians 1:9-10). It is a spiritual thing to discern which good works, of the 10,000 possible, are among the "every good work" that belong to my life and my church. Who of us can say that we have arrived when it comes to this matter of discerning best ministry decisions? And so I ask very earnestly: Do we have anything to learn from the fact that these deeply spiritual prophets and teachers worshiped and fasted as they sought the leading of the Lord?

Consider four simple observations from this story in Acts 13:1-4.

First, this fasting was *after* Christ's coming. I point this out lest someone say that fasting was a part of the Old Testament spirituality but not of New Testament spirituality. We have argued in Chapter One from Matthew 9:15 that Jesus expected that his disciples would fast when he had gone back to heaven. It is not surprising then to find them doing just that. Evidently Saul and Barnabas and the others in Antioch did not believe that fasting had passed like an old wineskin with the coming of the gospel and the new-covenant ministry of the Spirit.

Second, this fasting in Acts 13 was a corporate fast. At least five of them were united in this devotion to the Lord. I mention this because another concern with fasting is that Jesus warned against fasting to be seen by men (Matthew 6:17-18). He said, "But you, when you fast, anoint your head, and wash your face so that you may not be seen fasting by men, but by your Father who is in secret; and your Father who sees in secret will repay you" (Matthew 6:17-18). Yet it is impossible to fast corporately and not be seen by men. So the question is raised whether corporate fasting contradicts the teaching of Jesus. I argued in Chapter Three that it does not. And that is confirmed here by the practice of the apostle and church teachers. Saul and Barnabas evidently do not take Jesus to mean that corporate fasting is evil. The critical issue is not whether people know you are fasting but whether you want them to know so that you can bask in their admiration.

Third, this fasting in Acts 13 proved to be an occasion for the Spirit's special guidance. Verse 2 says, "And while they were ministering to the Lord and *fasting*, the Holy Spirit said, 'Set apart for Me Barnabas and Saul for the work to which I have called them.' Then, when they had *fasted* and prayed and laid their hands on them, they sent them away." In reporting it this

way, Luke clearly wants us to see a connection between the worship, prayer, and fasting on the one hand and the decisive guidance of the Holy Spirit on the other: "While they were fasting,
the Holy Spirit said." This is a significant biblical precedent for
engaging in worship-fasting-prayer in the earnest pursuit of
God's will for our lives and the life of our church.

Fourth, the fasting in Acts 13 changed the course of history.
It is almost impossible to overstate the historical importance of
that moment in the history of the world. Before this word from
the Holy Spirit, there seems to have been no organized mission
of the church beyond the eastern seacoast of the Mediterranean.
Before this, Paul had made no missionary journeys westward to
Asia Minor, Greece, Rome, or Spain. Before this Paul had not
written any of his letters, which were all a result of his missionary travels, which began here.

This moment of prayer and fasting resulted in a missions
movement that would catapult Christianity from obscurity into
being the dominant religion of the Roman Empire within two
and a half centuries, and would yield 1.3 billion adherents of the
Christian religion today, with a Christian witness in virtually
every country of the world. And thirteen out of the twenty-seven
books of the New Testament (Paul's letters) were a result of the
ministry that was launched in this historic moment of prayer and
fasting.

So I think it is fair to say that God was pleased to make worship and prayer and fasting the launching pad for a mission that
would change the course of world history. Is there a lesson here
for us?

God Had Moved Through Fasting Many Times Before

It had happened before, and it would happen again and again in
history. For example, in 2 Chronicles 20 the Moabites and

Ammonites and Meunites came against Jehoshaphat, the King of Judah. It was a terrifying horde of violent people coming against the people of the Lord. What could the people do? What direction should they turn? Verses 3-4 say, "Jehoshaphat was afraid and turned his attention to seek the Lord; and *proclaimed a fast* throughout all Judah. So Judah gathered together to seek help from the Lord; they even came from all the cities of Judah to seek the Lord."

So there was a great nationwide fast for divine guidance and deliverance. In the midst of that fasting assembly, according to verses 14-15, "the Spirit of the Lord came upon Jahaziel [the priest] . . . and he said, 'Listen, all Judah and the inhabitants of Jerusalem and King Jehoshaphat: thus says the Lord to you, "Do not fear or be dismayed because of this great multitude, for the battle is not yours but God's."'" The next day when the people of Judah went out, they found that the people of Moab and Ammon had destroyed one another, and it took Judah three days to gather the spoil.

The course of history was changed by the fasting of God's people. The stories of God's mighty grace through fasting are many. We could tell the story of Moses on Mount Sinai fasting forty days as he received the Law of God that would not only guide Israel for more than 3,000 years, but would become the foundation of Western culture as we know it (Exodus 24:18; 34:28). Or we could tell the story of how the Jews fasted for Esther as she risked her life before King Ahasuerus and turned the plot against Israel back on Haman's head (Esther 4:16). Or we could tell the story of Nehemiah's fasting for the sake of his people and the city of God in ruins, so that King Artaxerxes granted him all the help he needed to return and rebuild the walls of Jerusalem (Nehemiah 1:4). The course of history has been turned by many other factors besides fasting. I am not making any unique claims for this spiritual discipline. I only observe that

God, from time to time, has ordained that this be the means of changing the course of events for the good of his people.

A National Fast in Britain for Deliverance

And so it has continued after biblical times. John Wesley tells us in his journal of a similar kind of "biblical" deliverance in 1756. The king of Britain called for a day of solemn prayer and fasting because of a threatened invasion of the French. Wesley wrote,

> The fast day was a glorious day, such as London has scarce seen since the Restoration. Every church in the city was more than full, and a solemn seriousness sat on every face. Surely God heareth prayer, and there will yet be a lengthening of our tranquility.

Then in a footnote he added later, "Humility was turned into national rejoicing for the threatened invasion by the French was averted."[6]

The Rediscovery of Fasting in Our Own Day

There is in our own day a growing sense among many that the rediscovery of fasting as a penitential heart-cry to God for revival might be the means God would use to awaken and reform his church. Some have observed from Acts 13:1-4 there were three activities happening: these teachers and prophets were worshiping and praying and fasting. Of these three activities, two are experiencing worldwide resurgence in our day.

When we look around the world here at the end of the twentieth century, we see a remarkable worship awakening. Not all agree that the musical dimension of the awakening is an unmixed blessing either in lyrical quality or musical excellence. Nevertheless, who can deny that there are thousands of churches and movements praising the Lord with vitality and God-centered focus who twenty-five years ago did not put nearly such a premium on engaging with God in worship as they do today? Not only that, there is an amazing movement of prayer in our day. David Bryant documents this movement in *The Hope at Hand*, showing with dozens of illustrations that "God is stirring up his people to pray specifically, increasingly, and persistently for world revival."[7]

But of the three activities in Acts 13:1-4 (worship, prayer, and fasting), fasting has not had this kind of resurgence, except perhaps in a few places like South Korea. This has prompted some to ask: Might God not ordain that his fullest blessings will come to the church when we prevail in prayer with the intensity of fasting? That kind of intensification of prayer is what fasting is. It's a physical exclamation point at the end of the sentence, "We hunger for you, O God, to come in power." It's a cry with our body, not just our soul: "I really mean it, Lord! This much, I hunger for you. I want the manifestation of you yourself more than I want food."

Jonathan Edwards's Call for Fasting in the First Great Awakening

That this hunger for God should awaken a renewed interest in fasting is not new and not surprising. It has happened before at times of awakening. While the winds of the first Great Awakening in America were still blowing in 1742, Jonathan Edwards, its strongest defender and most penetrating analyst, longed for God to continue the blessing and increase it around the world. One of the means he commended was fasting:

> The state of the times extremely requires a fullness of the divine Spirit in ministers, and we ought to give ourselves no

rest till we have obtained it. And in order to [do] this, I should think ministers, above all persons, ought to be much in secret prayer and fasting, and also much in praying and fasting one with another. It seems to me it would be becoming the circumstances of the present day, if ministers in a neighborhood would often meet together and spend days in fasting and fervent prayer among themselves, earnestly seeking for those extraordinary supplies of divine grace from heaven, that we need at this day.[8]

One thing more I would mention concerning fasting and prayer, wherein I think there has been a neglect in ministers; and that is that although they recommend and much insist on the duty of secret prayer, in their preaching; so little is said about secret fasting. It is a duty recommended by our Savior to his followers, just in like manner as secret prayer is. . . . Though I don't suppose that secret fasting is to be practiced in a stated manner and steady course as secret prayer, yet it seems to me 'tis a duty that all professing Christians should practice, and frequently practice. There are many occasions of both a spiritual and temporal nature that do properly require it; and there are many particular mercies that we desire for ourselves or friends that it would be proper, in this manner, to seek of God.[9]

I should think the people of God in this land, at such a time as this is, would be in the way of their duty to do three times so much at fasting and prayer as they do.[10]

In our own day, voices are rising with a similar call for fasting and prayer for revival. But not everyone is as thoughtful and biblically careful as Edwards was in his wrestling with the realities of revival, in view of the lessons of history, the freedom and sovereignty of God, and the authority of Scripture over subjective impressions.

Edwards's Cautions for Our Contemporary Calls to Fast

Edwards hoped that this Great Awakening would be the final great movement of God's Spirit around the world that would usher in the golden age of gospel triumph before the coming of Christ. He said, "'Tis not unlikely that this work of God's Spirit, that is so extraordinary and wonderful, is the dawning, or at least a prelude, of that glorious work of God, so often foretold in Scripture, which in the progress and issue of it, shall renew the world of mankind."[11] It was not to be. Edwards was mistaken. But Edwards's view of God's freedom and sovereignty did not allow him to predict the scope of the revival, nor the date of its arrival, nor its global extent. Neither did its failure to come in the way he hoped cause him to be disillusioned with God or to grow weary in the cause of Truth.

There were those in his own day who went beyond his own hopes and his more careful expressions of what may probably be. They spoke from private revelations and subjective impressions of God's Spirit. Concerning these impressions about the revival Edwards sounded a warning that is relevant for our day.

> I would entreat the people of God to be very cautious how they give heed to such things. I have seen 'em fail in very many instances; and know by experience that impressions being made with great power, and upon the minds of true saints, yea, eminent saints; and presently after, yea, in the midst of, extraordinary exercises of grace and sweet communion with God, and attended with texts of scripture strongly impressed on the mind, are no sure signs of their being revelations from heaven: for I have known such impressions to fail, and prove vain by the event, in some instances attended with all these circumstances.[12]

What makes this warning so crucial is not only that subjective impressions are prevalent today regarding a possible coming revival, but also that Acts 13:1-4 seems to give us a model for seeking God's leading that involves subjective impressions. Recall that verse 2 says, "And while they were ministering to the Lord and fasting, *the Holy Spirit said*, 'Set apart for Me Barnabas and Saul for the work to which I have called them.'" How did the Holy Spirit "say" this? Well, we don't know. But it was not the only instance in Acts where the Spirit gave such direct guidance. For example, in Acts 8:29 we read, "And *the Spirit said to Philip*, 'Go up and join this chariot.'" Acts 10:19 says, "And while Peter was reflecting on the vision, *the Spirit said to him*, 'Behold, three men are looking for you. But arise, go downstairs, and accompany them.'"

Are there guidelines in the New Testament to help us discern if such a claim to hear the Spirit in our own day is truly from the Lord? This is not a simple question of whether one embraces charismatic viewpoints or not. Even mainline evangelicals claim to be "impressed by the Spirit" or "have a sense of God's leading" or think "God has placed it on their heart" to do a thing. The question is, how shall we test such claims, especially when it may involve a prediction about a coming revival or a call for the church to fast?

How Do We Test Subjective Impressions?

I would suggest several guidelines. First, we observe that in Acts 13:2 the Spirit spoke to five teachers and prophets as a group. Of course, the Spirit could speak to one person alone. But it would seem wise to say, where more people are obliged by a word from the Spirit, more people are informed about it by the Spirit. It does not seem to be the way of the Spirit in the New Testament to bind the consciences of Christians through the subjective impressions given to others. Apostolic authority binds our conscience to complete obedience (Galatians 1:12; 1 Corinthians 14:37-38;

2 Corinthians 10:8; 13:10; 1 Thessalonians 2:13; 2 Thessalonians 3:6; 2 Peter 3:1-2, 15-16). But other claims to divine leading must be "tested" (1 Thessalonians 5:21). This call for testing fits with the suggestion that where more people are obliged to follow, more people will be led to follow. It is not the solitary individual who constrains the body of Christ.

Second, the normative guidance in the New Testament follows the pattern of Romans 12:2, "Be transformed by the renewing of your mind, that you may prove what the will of God is, that which is good and acceptable and perfect." This need not rule out unusual impulses and impressions from the Lord, but it does suggest that the renewed "mind of Christ" (1 Corinthians 2:16), shaped by the word of Christ, and permeated by the Spirit of Christ, will hold sway in the interplay of subjective impression vs. spiritual reflection.

Third, the claim to have an impression from the Lord would need to conform to the teaching of Scripture, either to specific texts if any is immediately relevant, or to the tenor, spirit, and trajectory of the whole.

Fourth, the misuse of Scripture to support otherwise biblical impressions will give sober Christians pause. Sometimes private revelation is claimed for a specific call of God to the church which is not unbiblical, but for which the Scriptures are pressed into service they were never meant to have. This is an unlikely thing for the Spirit to do. He inspired the Scriptures and would, it seems, handle them according to the meaning that he gave them in the first place. Therefore, where the claim is made that the Spirit brought such and such a text to mind that is then misused, it may be doubted that the Spirit's leading is being accurately perceived.

Fifth, the larger track record of the person speaking is relevant. How accurately and helpfully has he or she discerned such impressions before? Has experience shown that God has entrusted this person with advance notice of his acts at other times? How stable and reliable is the person in general? Is there a broad biblical doctrinal base from which the person may be expected to be discerning of true and false thoughts that compete in all our minds for conviction?

Testing the Use of 2 Chronicles 7:14

This is my effort to give heed to Edwards's exhortation that we "be very cautious" with subjective impressions in our own day. For example, we should be careful with predictions in our own day to the effect that America will experience a great spiritual awakening by any particular date. This kind of prediction, so often repeated in the history of the church, can lead to great disillusionment, if God has another plan. More relevant for our immediate concern is the danger that subjective impressions may also from time to time dictate to the church that this or that spiritual discipline, like fasting, is *the* biblical key to revival. Edwards cautioned us that "texts of Scripture strongly impressed on the mind" of "eminent saints" is no sure sign of the use of these texts being accurate.

One of the texts most commonly cited in the hope for imminent revival is 2 Chronicles 7:14, "[If] My people who are called by My name humble themselves and pray, and seek My face and turn from their wicked ways, then I will hear from heaven, will forgive their sin, and will heal their land." Mistaken uses of this verse lessen our confidence in the predictions some make concerning a coming revival.

First, in the original context where God speaks these words to Solomon, the term "my people" refers to the people of Israel, and therefore the term "their land" refers to a land that is really "theirs" in the sense of God's giving it to them as a covenant blessing, namely, the land of Israel. But when we apply this text to our contemporary situation, "my people" would refer to the

Christian Church who cannot say, in whatever country that they reside, that this country is "their land." The church has no land, the way Israel had a land. The Christian Church is a pilgrim people. We are aliens and exiles (1 Peter 2:11). Therefore, the proper application of 2 Chronicles 7:14 would, perhaps, be that, if the church will humble herself and pray and seek God's face and turn from her wicked ways, God will incline to heal *the church*. But it goes beyond what this text assures if we say that any country where the Christian church humbles herself will experience a Great Awakening.

Another mistake would be to elevate any one spiritual discipline as *the* decisive key to such an awakening. Biblical and historical precedent would encourage us to seek revival and awakening and reformation through prayer and fasting. But that same precedent would discourage us from making any one spiritual activity the key that must unlock the awakening we seek. It would be especially misleading to attach fasting, for example, to 2 Chronicles 7:14 as a certain way of fulfilling this verse—for at least three reasons.

One reason is that 2 Chronicles 7:14 does not mention fasting. A second reason is that the further references in 2 Chronicles where God blesses those who humble themselves according to 2 Chronicles 7:14 do not all involve fasting (12:6-7, 12; 32:26; 33:12-13, 19; 34:27). This is not at all to deny that fasting would be a legitimate way to humble ourselves before the Lord, but simply to say that there is no biblical warrant for thinking that this verse is a call to fast. The third reason for not connecting fasting to 2 Chronicles 7:14 as the key to this verse is that it is possible to do extraordinary fasting and yet not humble ourselves, pray, seek God, and turn from wickedness. This is plain from numerous texts. For example:

*When they fast, I am not going to listen to their cry; and
when they offer burnt offering and grain offering, I am not
going to accept them. Rather I am going to make an end of
them by the sword, famine and pestilence.*
—Jeremiah 14:12

*Say to all the people of the land and to the priests, "When
you fasted and mourned in the fifth and seventh months
these seventy years, was it actually for Me that you fasted?"*
—Zechariah 7:5

*"Why have we fasted and Thou dost not see? Why have we
humbled ourselves and Thou dost not notice?" Behold, on
the day of your fast you find your desire, and drive hard all
your workers.*
—Isaiah 58:3

The Ambiguity of Fasting

All of these passages are designed to caution us not to elevate any
outward ritual, like fasting, to the level of a sure key to unlock
revival. God is free to send revival with or without fasting.
Jonathan Edwards longed for revival as much as anyone, and he
called for prayer and fasting loud and clear. Yet he also discov-
ered something profound in his own experience about the freedom of God's sovereignty. He wrote,

How often we have mocked God with hypocritical pretenses
of humiliation, as in our annual days of public fasting and
other things, while instead of reforming, we only grew worse
and worse; how dead a time it was everywhere before this
work began. If we consider these things, we shall be most
stupidly ungrateful, if we don't acknowledge God's visiting
of us as he has done, as an instance of the glorious triumph
of free and sovereign grace.[13]

His point here is that public fasting and other rigors had gone on for a long time, yet were full of pretense and deadness. The people were not "turning from their wicked ways" while they fasted. They were not "seeking God's face" from the heart as they fasted. But suddenly, as the wind that blows where it wills (John 3:8), revival came. From this Edwards concludes that revival is "an instance of the glorious triumph of free and sovereign grace." That is what it was then, and that is what it will be when and if it comes today. And may God grant that it come!

The Passion of Edwards and Brainerd

For all of Jonathan Edwards's cautions about the misuse of subjective impressions in promoting fasting (or anything else), he had no hesitation in extolling the importance of it in the mission and ministry of the church. Besides the call to prayer and fasting quoted earlier, there is the long and painful account of his friend, the young missionary to the Indians, David Brainerd.

David Brainerd was born on April 20, 1718, in Haddam, Connecticut. That year John Wesley and Jonathan Edwards turned fourteen. Benjamin Franklin turned twelve and George Whitefield three. The Great Awakening was just over the horizon, and Brainerd would live through both waves of it in the mid-thirties and early forties, then die of tuberculosis in Jonathan Edwards's house at the age of twenty-nine on October 9, 1747. Jonathan held this young man in such esteem that he took pains to preserve and edit his journals and diary. Here is where we see Brainerd's and Edwards's views of the importance of fasting.

For example, on the analogy of Acts 13:1-4, Brainerd sought the guidance of the Lord for his ministry through regular times of fasting.

Monday, April 19. I set apart this day for fasting and prayer to God for his grace, especially to prepare me for the work of the ministry, *to give me divine aid and direction in my preparations for that great work,* and in his own time to 'send me into his harvest'. Accordingly, in morning, endeavored to plead for the divine presence for the day, and not without some life. In the forenoon, I felt a power of intercession for precious immortal souls, for the advancement of the kingdom of my dear Lord and Savior in the world; and withal, a most sweet resignation, and even consolation and joy in the thoughts of suffering hardships, distresses, and even death itself, in the promotion of it; and had special enlargement in pleading for the enlightening and conversion of the poor heathen.[14]

For Edwards this use of fasting was not only praiseworthy for missionaries like Brainerd, but also for "ministers and private Christians." It was in fact the means of continual blessing in Brainerd's life and might be in our own as well.

His example and success with regard to one duty in special may be of great use to *both ministers and private Christians;* I mean, the duty of secret fasting. The reader has seen how much Mr. Brainerd recommends this duty, and how frequently he exercised himself in it; nor can it well have escaped observation how much he was owned and blessed in it, and of what great benefit it evidently was to his soul. Among all the many days he spent in secret fasting and prayer that he gives an account of in his diary, there is scarce an instance of one but what was either attended or soon followed with *apparent success and a remarkable blessing in special incomes and consolations of God's Spirit;* and very often before the day was ended.[15]

This is why Edwards pleaded with pastors and laypeople of his day to give themselves with triple diligence (see above) to the discipline of prayer and fasting. It had proved for Brainerd and for hundreds of others in the history of the church to be a means of "remarkable blessing and . . . special incomes and consolations of God's Spirit." In other words, fasting had proved to be a pathway to awakening and revival.

A Plea for Pastors from a Puritan Shepard

One other illustration of this strong commitment to fasting as the pathway to vital Christianity comes from the century prior to Jonathan Edwards in New England. Thomas Shepard was born in England in 1605 and came to America in 1635. As a pastor in New England he preached a series of messages that was published as *The Parable of the Ten Virgins*, which is significant because Jonathan Edwards quoted this book more than any other in writing his masterpiece called *Treatise Concerning the Religious Affections*. Cotton Mather, who lived from 1663 to 1727, preserved the stories of many early New England ministers including the life of Thomas Shepard. His recollections reveal some of the roots of Edwards's deep commitment to fasting as part of the ministerial life and a pathway to revival. Mather invites us into Thomas Shepard's study:

> If we follow him unto his beloved study, there we shall find him affording yet a more notable and eminent instance of an holy walk. Here, besides his daily supplications, he did one thing which had a mighty tendency to keep his own spirit in an healthy, vigorous, thriving temper, and bringing down the manifold blessings of God upon all the weighty concerns, which he had in his hands; and a thing it was, without which he thought he could never prove either a watchful Christian or a very useful minister; this was *that he scarce permitted one month to pass him, without spending at least one day in the exercises of a secret-fast before the Lord*. It is remark-

able that every one of those three who are famous in the book of God for miraculous fasting [Moses, Elijah, Jesus], were honored by God with the miraculous feeding of other men. Our [Rev.] *Shepard thought that he should never do any great things in feeding of his flock, if he did not great things in fasting by himself.*[16]

Mather himself clearly endorses this commitment to fasting and longed for a great awakening in his own day. Interestingly Mather's eschatology was different from Edwards's, but both hoped and prayed and fasted for awakening. Edwards was a post-millennialist, and Mather was a premillennialist. Edwards prayed for a great awakening that would issue in a golden era of Christian dominance in the world before Christ's return. "Mather was convinced that Christ's imminent return would be preceded both by the extensive spiritual decline which he saw in New England, and European Protestantism, and by extraordinary outpourings of the Holy Spirit producing bright spots of revival and world missions, and especially the ingathering of Jewish converts."[17]

This is doubly encouraging today. It points the way across relatively minor doctrinal differences toward united prayer and fasting for the sake of the revival and reformation of God's people and the awakening of our spiritually dead American landscape. It even points the way to a common prayer-hope, even if we do not agree on the precise end-time scenario.

Most Encouraging of All

And perhaps most hopeful of all is this: Cotton Mather died in 1727 just before the winds of the first Great Awakening in America were about to blow. Richard Lovelace points out that Mather's hope for widespread awakening flagged just at the end of his life.[18] If he could only have seen what a decade would bring! May the Lord grant that our passion for God's supremacy in all things for the joy of all peoples may not weaken, but only grow and intensify through fasting and prayer. And may God indeed raise up millions who are so hungry for him that they cannot but cry out from body and soul: "This much, O God, this much, we long for your fullness in the church and your glory in the world!"

Is this not the fast which I choose,
To loosen the bonds of wickedness,
To undo the bands of the yoke,
And to let the oppressed go free,
And break every yoke?
Is it not to divide your bread with the hungry,
And bring the homeless poor into the house;
When you see the naked, to cover him;
And not to hide yourself from your own flesh?
Then your light will break out like the dawn,
And your recovery will speedily spring forth;
And your righteousness will go before you;
The glory of the LORD will be your rear guard.

—ISAIAH 58:6-8

About a billion of the world's people live in conditions of absolute poverty without even the most basic resources available—no adequate food, clothing, shelter, or medical care. 400 million are severely malnourished, including more than 200 million children.

—LARRY LIBBY
The Cry of the Poor[1]

6

FINDING GOD IN
THE GARDEN OF PAIN

*A Different Fast for
the Sake of the Poor*

One of the greatest preachers of the first thousand years of the
Christian Church was John Chrysostom, the bishop of Constantinople in the fourth century. He has left us one of the most sweeping statements I know concerning the value of fasting. He was
known as an ascetic in an age of luxury in Constantinople. His
lifestyle offended the emperor Arcadius and his wife Eudoxia so
much that he was eventually banished and died in A.D. 407.
Chrysostom therefore embodied, it seems, not only the discipline
of fasting but also the commitments to holy living that, as we will
see in a moment, are an even greater fast than going without food.

> Fasting is, as much as lies in us, an imitation of the angels, a
> contemning of things present, a school of prayer, a nourish-
> ment of the soul, a bridle of the mouth, an abatement of con-
> cupiscence: it mollifies rage, it appeases anger, it calms the
> tempests of nature, it excites reason, it clears the mind, it dis-
> burdens the flesh, it chases away night-pollutions, it frees
> from head-ache. By fasting, a man gets composed behaviour,
> free utterance of his tongue, right apprehensions of his mind.[2]

I take Chrysostom to mean that fasting has had these good effects on him and others from time to time, not that it always does, nor that it assists everyone with all these benefits. For example, for some people fasting will (at least temporarily) *cause* a headache rather than take it away. Nevertheless, thousands have heard the word of the Lord in Matthew 9:15 that "when the Bridegroom is taken away, then [his disciples] will fast," and they have proven its immense spiritual value. The more you read in the history of fasting, the more varied appear the testimonies to its benefits. (See Appendix: "Fasting: Quotes and Experiences.")

The Dangers of Fasting

However, what we have already seen, and will now see again, is that there is danger in fasting. I'm not referring to physical danger. You can avoid that if you follow simple guidelines.[3] I am referring to spiritual dangers. It is possible to fast in a way that will be very displeasing to the Lord and spiritually destructive to yourself.

If you fast, for example, to be seen by other people, Jesus said, you have your reward from them, and you will not be answered by the Father (Matthew 6:16). To test our motives, he said that we should take steps not to be seen by others, but only by God: comb your hair, wash your face, and do not put on an oh-poor-me countenance. Then—if your motives are pure—your Father who sees in secret will reward you.

Fasting and the Suffering of the City

But that is not the only warning about fasting in the Bible. The prophet Isaiah delivers a strong word that has tremendous relevance for our day. For me, as well as others, it has proved to be a very personal word. I live and minister in the city. I am surrounded by the kind of human calamity that accumulates at urban centers. I live continually with the question of how my faith—including fasting—relates to these realities. Isaiah 58 has awakened in me, and many in my church, a passion to spend and be spent for the good of those in greatest need. It has functioned more than once to give us our bearings as a church when we ponder what it means to spread a passion for the supremacy of God in all things in the center of the city.

> Cry loudly, do not hold back;
>> Raise your voice like a trumpet,
> And declare to My people their transgression,
>> And to the house of Jacob their sins.
> Yet they seek Me day by day,
>> and delight to know My ways,
> As a nation that has done righteousness,
>> And has not forsaken the ordinance of their God.
> They ask Me for just decisions,
>> They delight in the nearness of God.
> "Why have we fasted and Thou dost not see?
>> Why have we humbled ourselves
>> and Thou dost not notice?"
> Behold, on the day of your fast
>> you find your desire,
>> And drive hard all your workers.
> Behold, you fast for contention and strife
>> and to strike with a wicked fist.
> You do not fast like you do today
>> to make your voice heard on high.
> Is it a fast like this which I choose,
>> a day for a man to humble himself?
> Is it for bowing one's head like a reed,
>> And for spreading out sackcloth and ashes as a bed?
> Will you call this a fast,
>> even an acceptable day to the LORD?

Is this not the fast which I choose,
    To loosen the bonds of wickedness,
To undo the bands of the yoke,
    And to let the oppressed go free,
And break every yoke?
Is it not to divide your bread with the hungry,
    And bring the homeless poor into the house;
When you see the naked, to cover him;
    And not to hide yourself from your own flesh?
Then your light will break out like the dawn,
    And your recovery will speedily spring forth;
And your righteousness will go before you;
    The glory of the LORD will be your rear guard.
Then you will call, and the LORD will answer;
    You will cry, and He will say, "Here I am."
If you remove the yoke from your midst,
    The pointing of the finger, and speaking wickedness,
And if you give yourself to the hungry,
    And satisfy the desire of the afflicted,
Then your light will rise in darkness,
    And your gloom will become like midday.
And the LORD will continually guide you,
    And satisfy your desire in scorched places,
And give strength to your bones;
    And you will be like a watered garden,
And like a spring of water whose waters do not fail.
    And those from among you will rebuild the ancient ruins;
You will raise up the age-old foundations;
    And you will be called the repairer of the breach,
The restorer of the streets in which to dwell.

Bill Leslie Discovers the Watered Garden

Those of us in my church are not the only ones who have heard a personal word from God in Isaiah 58. I recall a testimony from Bill Leslie, the former pastor of LaSalle Street Church in

Chicago, who had a long and remarkable ministry in the city, not unlike the one described in Isaiah 58. He came to Minneapolis once and told of a near breakdown that he had had and how a spiritual mentor directed him to this chapter. He said it was verse 11 that saved him from a dead-end street of exhaustion and burnout.

> ¹⁰*And if you give yourself to the hungry,*
>   *And satisfy the desire of the afflicted,*
> *Then your light will rise in darkness,*
>   *And your gloom will become like midday.*
> ¹¹ *And the LORD will continually guide you,*
>   *And satisfy your desire in scorched places*
>   [like urban Chicago]
> *And give strength to your bones;*
>   And you will be like a watered garden,
>   And like a spring of water whose waters do not fail.

What struck Pastor Leslie so powerfully was the fact that God promises to make us like a watered garden (not just a watering ministry, but a watered ministry). That is, we will receive the water we need for refreshment, and we will become a spring of water that does not fail—for others—for the demanding, exhausting, draining ministry of urban self-giving. This gave him a pattern of divine life that got him through his crisis and kept him going for years more. The amazing thing we need to see here is that Isaiah calls this experience of being watered as a garden for others a kind of fasting.

Divide Your Bread with the Hungry
Even When You Have Cancer

There is at least one other experience I have had with this text that makes it so personally compelling. Doug Nichols is presently the president of Action International Ministries, a mission that focuses especially on the millions of street children in the big cities of the world. He is the kind of man who calls our church staff on the phone during an international crisis and suggests that we rent a jumbo jet and take a couple hundred of our people to Rwanda to help bury the dead so that doctors and nurses can do what they were sent to do. He is relentlessly focussed on pouring out his life for the helpless who need Christ.

For example, he writes to me every now and then, and almost always includes some sword thrust like this in a P.S. at the bottom of his letter: "In the last 'one minute' that it possibly took you to read this letter, 28 children died of malnutrition and diseases that could have been easily prevented. 1,667 die every hour, 40,000 children die daily! Please pray with ACTION for more missionaries to take the gospel to these children."

Doug was found to have colon cancer in April of 1993. Doctors gave him a 30% chance of living after his surgery and colostomy and radiation treatments. During horrible civil war between the Hutus and the Tutsis, he got on a plane and went to Rwanda with a team of people, including some from our church. His non-Christian oncologist said he would die in Rwanda. Doug said that would be OK because he is going to heaven. The oncologist was distressed and called Doug's surgeon to solicit help in restraining Doug from going to Rwanda. The surgeon, who is a Christian, said that Doug was ready to die and go to heaven.

When we got word here that Doug was going—with his cancer and his colostomy—to Rwanda, some of us on the staff gathered in the prayer room to pray for him. I recall being led very specifically to Isaiah 58:7-8, which we prayed for Doug.

[Is the fast I choose] not to divide your bread with the hungry,
  And bring the homeless poor into the house;
  When you see the naked, to cover him;

And not to hide yourself from your own flesh?
Then your light will break out like the dawn,
And your recovery [your healing!] *will speedily spring forth;*

We prayed very specifically that the feeding of the hungry and the housing of the homeless in Rwanda would not kill Doug Nichols, but would heal him. From Rwanda, Doug called his oncologist and said he was not dead. And when he got back he had a battery of tests that resulted in the assessment NED: no evidence of disease. God alone holds the future for Doug Nichols and his remarkable faith and ministry, but for now Isaiah 58 lives bodily in Doug's life as he pours himself out for the children.

So you can see that Isaiah 58 has some very significant associations in my life. The fasting that it calls for is no ordinary kind. And I am praying that the stories of its life-changing power will be multiplied through this book.

Jesus Loved This Prophet

There is something very close to Jesus' heart in Isaiah 58. You can hear it coming out in Jesus' words in Luke 4:18 ("The Spirit of the Lord is upon Me, because He anointed Me to preach the gospel to the poor. He has sent Me to proclaim release to the captives, and recovery of sight to the blind, to set free those who are downtrodden") and in Matthew 25:35 ("I was hungry, and you gave Me something to eat; I was thirsty, and you gave Me drink; I was a stranger, and you invited Me in; naked, and you clothed Me; I was sick, and you visited Me; I was in prison, and you came to Me") and John 7:38 ("He who believes in Me, as the Scripture said, 'From his innermost being shall flow rivers of living water'"). The burden of Isaiah 58 pervades the ministry of Jesus—and more and more it should pervade our ministry as well.

Fasting as Veneer for Vice

In the first three verses, God brings an indictment against his people. He tells Isaiah to cry loudly and declare to the house of Jacob their sins. But their sins are cloaked with an amazing veneer of religious fervor. This is what is so stunning and sobering, especially for us who are religious and who practice religious disciplines like fasting. Listen to the indictment: "Yet they seek Me day by day, and delight to know My ways, as [that is, as if they were] a nation that has done righteousness, and has not forsaken the ordinance of their God" (verse 2). In other words, they act as if they are a righteous and obedient nation. And they persuade themselves that they really want God and his ways. This is a terrible kind of delusion to live in.

He goes on near the end of verse 3: "They ask Me for just decisions, they delight in the nearness of God." But they are not sincere. They want God to intervene for them with righteous judgments, because things are not going well, as we will see in a moment. But they do not see the real problem. They love to come to worship. They talk the language of the nearness of God. They may even have moving religious and aesthetic experiences in their efforts to draw near to God. But something is wrong.

Beware Loving Loving God Rather Than Loving God

This is a very relevant warning for us in a day of great worship renewal. Many people are discovering the joy of meeting God in extended times of emotionally charged singing to the Lord. I personally find such seasons of lingering before the Lord a very rich communion with him. But I see a danger. The danger is that we will subtly slip from loving God in these moments into loving loving God. That's the way one of my colleagues put it recently. In other words, we begin to savor not the glory of

God but the atmosphere created by worship. When this happens we open ourselves to hypocrisy. And under the cloak of great religious fervor, deadly inconsistencies can emerge in our lives.

It All Looked So Good

Something is wrong in the worship of Isaiah 58. The people express their frustration in verse 3, but they don't know what is wrong. They say to God, "Why have we fasted and Thou dost not see? Why have we humbled [or afflicted] ourselves and Thou dost not notice?" In fact, verses 2 and 3 mention five religious activities they are doing in vain. In verse 2 it says (1) they are seeking God; (2) they delight to know God's ways; (3) they ask God for just decisions; and (4) they delight in the nearness of God. Then in verse 3, they are (5) fasting and afflicting themselves. Yet, in spite of all of that, God tells Isaiah, "Cry loudly [not softly, not quietly, but loudly] . . . and declare to my people their transgression" (verse 1).

They were fasting. They were seeking God's face. They were praying. They were doing a kind of external humbling of themselves. This all sounds just like what we are supposed to do, according to 2 Chronicles 7:14. Nevertheless, this fasting and this worship is not pleasing to the Lord. It is the kind of fasting and worship we do not want. And yet, we ask, what is wrong with seeking God, and delighting to know his ways, and asking him for just decisions, and delighting in his nearness, and fasting and humbling ourselves before him? What is wrong with that? It sounds like the very way we talk about worship at its best! Is that not sobering? Does that that not make us tremble? Does it not make us want to get so real with God that we could never be startled by the Lord in this way—with our most zealous religious practices and desires exposed as a sham?

What's wrong with their worship? God answers:

> Behold, on the day of your fast
>   you find your desire,
>   And drive hard all your workers.
> Behold, you fast for contention and strife
>   and to strike with a wicked fist.
> You do not fast like you do today
>   to make your voice heard on high.
> Is it a fast like this which I choose,
>   a day for a man to humble himself?
> Is it for bowing one's head like a reed,
>   And for spreading out sackcloth and ashes as a bed?
> Will you call this a fast,
>   even an acceptable day to the LORD? (verses 3b-5)

So here's the issue. The ethical, practical, relational accompaniments of fasting are the real test of the authenticity of the fasting. God lists the external religious forms of fasting: humbling or afflicting oneself (no food), bowing the head like a reed, spreading out sackcloth and ashes. Then he lists the (un)ethical accompaniments of fasting: you go after your own pleasure (in some other way besides eating), you drive hard all your workers; you become irritable or contentious and stir up strife; and you even go so far as to get into fights. And God asks, "Is this the fast that I choose?" The answer is No.

The Paradox of Self-indulgent Fasting

So here we have another test of whether fasting is authentic or not. Jesus said, If you are fasting to be seen by others you have your reward. Isaiah says, If your fasting leaves you self-indulgent in other areas, harsh toward your employees, irritable and contentious, then your fasting is not acceptable to God. So God is mercifully warning us against the danger of substituting religious disciplines for righteous living.

Oh, how we need to ponder these things. Hypocrisy is a terrible blight on the worship of God. Let us take to heart the long-term implications for worship in our lives and in our churches. No worship—no preaching, no singing, no praying, no fasting, however intense or beautiful—that leaves us harsh with our workers on Monday, or contentious with our spouses at home, or self-indulgent in other areas of our lives, or angry enough to hit somebody, is true, God-pleasing worship. Don't make a mistake here: true fasting may be a God-blessed means of overcoming harshness at work, and contentiousness at home, and self-indulgence and anger. But if fasting ever becomes a religious cloak for minimizing those things and letting them go on and on, then it becomes hypocrisy and offensive to God.

Monday's Work Proves Sunday's Worship

How you treat people on Monday is the test of the authenticity of your fasting on Sunday. Fasting that leaves our daily lives unchanged in sin is the butt of God's ridicule: "Is it a fast like this . . . for bowing one's head like a reed?" (verse 5). In other words, the gestures of such fasting are no more spiritual than a bent reed in the swamp.

Woe to the fasting that leaves sin in our lives untouched. The only authentic fasting is fasting that includes a spiritual attack against our own sin. Is our fasting really a hunger for God? We test whether it is by whether we are hungering for our own holiness. To want God is to hate sin. For God is holy, and we cannot love God and love sin. Fasting that is not aimed at starving sin while feasting on God is self-deluded. It is not really God that we hunger for in such fasting. The hunger of fasting is a hunger for God, and the test of that hunger is whether it includes a hunger for holiness.

Fasting Is Meant to Starve Sin, Not Us

If there is an unresolved pocket of sin in our life and we are fasting, instead, about something else, God is going to come to us and say, "The fast that I choose is for *that sin* to be starved to death." The way he does that in Isaiah 58 is very striking. Isaiah says in verse 5 that they were fasting and "humbling themselves." That word "humbling" also means "afflicting." So they were afflicting themselves with hunger. But God says that this is not the fast he chooses. Then, in verse 10, he takes these very words "hungry" and "afflicted" and says that there are some hungry and afflicted people that he is indeed concerned about—namely, the ones who have no choice but to be hungry and afflicted, because the fasting folks oppress them instead of feeding them.

> And if you give yourself to the hungry,
> And satisfy the desire of the afflicted . . .

In other words, God says, your fasting and self-affliction is not really an attack on your own sin of injustice and hardheartedness. If they were, your action would be to alleviate the hunger and affliction of your workers. There is a great irony here that God wants us to see. The poor are hungry and afflicted, verse 10 says. These well-to-do religious people are also hungry and afflicted—with fasting. But what are they fasting for? Is their fasting first a battle against their own sin—the sin of driving hard all their workers? The sin of putting a heavy yoke on the back of the poor? The sin of neglecting their clothing needs and housing needs? No. That is not what they are fasting against. Their behavior proves it.

So God comes to them and says, The fast that I choose is not that you religiously make yourselves hungry and afflicted, but that you make the poor less hungry and afflicted. If you want to fight sin by taking bread away from your own mouth, then put it in the mouth of the poor. Then we will see if you are really fasting for righteousness' sake.

When we are living in sin, the fast that God chooses is not a religious covering, but a direct frontal assault. For these people, fasting was not a fight against the besetting sin of their lives; it was a camouflage. If they make themselves hunger a little bit and afflict themselves a little bit, maybe it won't matter so much that they are indifferent to the hunger and the affliction of the poor. So God comes and says, I test your hearts. Go without bread for the sake of the poor. That's the fast I choose.

Consumerism and the American Inner-city Kid

Fasting in America and other prosperous western nations is almost incomprehensible because we are brainwashed by a consumer culture. We are taught to experience the good life by consuming, not by renouncing consumption. As Rodney Clapp puts it, "The consumer is schooled in insatiability. . . . The consumer is tutored that people basically consist of unmet needs that can be appeased by commodified goods and experiences. Accordingly, the consumer should think first and foremost of himself or herself and meeting his or her felt needs."[4] That it might be more blessed to give rather than to receive (Acts 20:35) is almost inconceivable. Therefore fasting is barely thinkable except as a weight loss fad or a New-Age enhancement for higher consciousness—both of which are embedded in a consumer culture.

The pervasiveness of consumerism is manifest starkly when we realize how deeply it permeates all levels of society, even those that can scarcely afford to consume. The mark of consumer culture is the reduction of "being" to "having." And this reduction is fed daily by television. Even in the inner city among the poor who cannot afford very much, teenagers

are connoisseurs of pop culture, ready receptacles for the jingles and scattershot imagery of television. Their speech is drenched in the verbal flotsam of television shows. . . . On the street, being a person of "substance" is defined ironically as having a certain appearance or image. . . . [One teenage boy] quickly quits his summer job bagging groceries when he realizes it threatens his image. He spends the first 75 dollars he earns from another job on a beeper, in part because it makes him look like a drug dealer [even though he has] nothing to do with drugs. . . . [He] also periodically carries a gun and peddles stolen merchandise: such acts prove that he is not a "wuss" but a person of "substance.". . . [He] and his friends call themselves "LoLifes" (short for "Polo Lifes") because they wear only Polo brand men's clothing, most of it stolen from department stores downtown. . . . [He] believes that "clothes make the man." Tragically, in his case, the maxim is chillingly accurate. . . . When the designer clothes are stripped away, we find virtually no substance behind the appearance. [He] has been reduced to a mere acquirer of goods and consumer of products. . . . [He and his friends] "trust what they have been told about image, status, competition, hierarchy, and the primacy of self-gratification. Their faith is lethal, mostly to themselves."[5]

This inner-city kid and his friends are a stark portrayal of mainstream America, minus the softening effects of wealth.

Many mainstream Americans have an idolatrous faith in materialism, but it is tempered by the opportunities they have (educationally and vocationally) to build their identities on something other than their appearance. While they too are consumers, they have the opportunity to become more than mere consumers. By contrast [our inner-city kid] and his friends cannot or will not access such opportunities. Consequently, "meaning" gets hollowed out of their world and replaced with "image." In this shrunken existence, kids literally kill each other for gold chains and leather jackets. . . . The kids' blind faith in consumerism is fatal.[6]

Against this backdrop of the pervasive contemporary American consumerism, the fasting of Isaiah 58 begins to have a sharper point. That a lifestyle of serving the poor rather than consuming another commodity should be called a "fast" is not so strange after all. Most of our life is a gorging of one artificially inflamed appetite after another. Any alteration of this pattern for the sake of ministry is a "fast"—and one that would please God more than a hundred skipped lunches with a view to more pizza at supper.

The Non-negotiable Living Fast of Love

What God does now in Isaiah 58:6-12 is describe what is involved in living out this fast and what the spectacular rewards are for living this way—that it really is more blessed to give than to receive, in ways we can't even imagine from inside our consumer addictions. You recall that Jesus said, "Your heavenly Father who sees in secret will reward you." Well, here are some of the kinds of things God promises for those who do this kind of fasting.

First look at the description of the fasting itself. Then we will look at the promises of God for those who live this way. Don't make the mistake of thinking this is a job description that God had given his people to show them how to earn wages from him. There is no earning going on here. The God of Isaiah cannot be negotiated with. He is sovereign and free and gives graciously to those who trust him. Isaiah 30:15 says, "For thus the

Lord God, the Holy One of Israel, has said, 'In repentance and rest you shall be saved, in quietness and trust is your strength.'" The strength to do what God calls us to do does not come from us. It comes from God, and it comes through trusting him.

This Fast Is the Doctor's Prescription

When God tells the people what to do, this is not a job *description*, but a doctor's *prescription*. He is not telling us to earn wages by laboring for a boss, but to get well by trusting our Physician. You can see this in verse 8 where it says, if you follow God's word, "Your recovery [your healing!] will speedily spring forth." If you trust the doctor and show your trust by obeying his instructions, you will get well from your sickness of sin. So don't think that you are going to earn anything from God. That is impossible, and deadly to try. Trust his sovereign grace and follow his counsel, and you will be mightily blessed. But it will never occur to you to think that you have earned or merited anything.

So let's look at God's *prescription* here—the fast that God chooses. Beginning in verse 6:

> Is not this the fast I choose,
> To loosen the bonds of wickedness,
>   To undo the bands of the yoke,
> And to let the oppressed go free,
>   And break every yoke?
> Is it not to divide your bread with the hungry,
>   And bring the homeless poor into the house;
> When you see the naked, to cover him;
>   And not to hide yourself from your own flesh?

Then in verses 8 and 9a come the *promises* of what will happen if we trust the doctor's prescription on how to fast. But skip over that for a moment and go to the rest of the prescription in verse 9b-10a.

> *If you remove the yoke from your midst,*
>   *The pointing of the finger,*
> *and speaking wickedness,*
>   *And if you give yourself to the hungry,*
>   *And satisfy the desire of the afflicted . . .*

That's the doctor's prescription. That's the fast that the doctor prescribes for the patient Israel, who is sick with the disease of hypocrisy and hardheartedness—and for the prosperous modern American who is sick with the addictions of consumerism.

There are thirteen components, but they seem to fall into seven categories. I take each of them as a personal call on my own life and as a mandate for the church. This is the fasting I must learn and enjoy. This is the remedy for the modern pseudo-freedom of unending commodity choices that clog my heart with things—like 30,000 products in the average American supermarket in 1996 as opposed to 9,000 in 1975, or one new periodical for every day of the year, or thirty TV stations to choose from each night.[7]

First, God prescribes that we set people free.

> *To loosen the bonds of wickedness,*
>   *To undo the bands of the yoke,*
> *And to let the oppressed go free,*
>   *And break every yoke. . . . (verse 6)*
> *If you remove the yoke from your midst . . . (verse 9)*

Bonds, bands, yoke, oppression, yoke, yoke . . . The point here is this: let us live to free people, not to burden them. Jesus said in Luke 11:46, "Woe to you lawyers as well! For you weigh men down with burdens hard to bear, while you yourselves will not even touch the burdens with one of your fingers." There is a burden and a yoke we should offer people, but it is a light burden and an easy yoke. Jesus said, "Come to Me, all who are weary and heavy-laden, and I will give you rest. Take My yoke upon you, and learn from Me, for I am gentle and humble in heart; and you shall find rest for your souls. For My yoke is easy, and My load is light" (Matthew 11:28-30). Jesus calls us to join him in freeing people from heavy burdens and hard yokes.

What makes his burden light is the reality of the new birth that changes what we love to do, from the inside out (as 1 John 5:3-4 says): "For this is the love of God, that we keep His commandments; and His commandments are *not burdensome*. For whatever is *born of God* overcomes the world." Being born of God triumphs over the worldly cravings that make the commandments of God burdensome. Thus the prescribed fast begins with the new birth and yields new values and desires that bear fruit in freedom and joy. This is God's prescribed fast.

I received an E-mail from a missionary friend in a restricted-access country whose presence there hangs in part on the "humanitarian assistance" he brings. But he is experiencing first-hand the necessity of prior spiritual transformation before humanitarian transformation can take hold. He writes,

> In a nutshell, [the government] has decided to cut all funding for the business center and pump it into the "orphanage." That sounds wonderful except for one thing. They've made the funding of the orphanage contingent on changing its clientele. They are demanding that the school be started not just for orphans, but run as an English school for orphans and a few "gifted" students who are not orphans. Of course, they want American "volunteers" to teach at this school. The few "gifted" students would just so happen to come from among the children of the very government officials who are provid-

ing the funding! Discouraging, isn't it? This is exactly the reason why reforming a culture must begin at the spiritual end (church-planting), not with "humanitarian assistance."

Second, God prescribes that we feed the hungry.

> *Is [this fast] not to divide your bread*
> *with the hungry? (verse 7a)*

Our fast is not merely to deny ourselves but to supply the needs of others. About 40,000 children a day die from hunger and from easily preventable childhood diseases. "About a billion of the world's people live in conditions of absolute poverty without even the most basic resources available—no adequate food, clothing, shelter, or medical care. . . . 400 million are severely malnourished—including more than 200 million children."[8]

These facts, plus the ones just outside my door, are relevant to how I fast. God will not allow me to content myself with severe discipline that does not attack the oblivion in which most comfortable middle-class Americans live. He says that fasting is meant to awaken us to the hunger of the world, not just our own hunger. And he says it is a heart-cry not just to savor the goodness of God in our own bounty, but in the power of love to live for the sake of others.

Do not be paralyzed by the statistics. We are not responsible for what we cannot do but for what we can do. And there are hundreds of do-able things for those who take their fast seriously. A simple example from Manila. "Smokey Mountain" is the well-known city of trash where Manila's garbage is dumped, and where 15,000 squatters and their families live by savaging the leftovers from the city.

Primary health care workers with Youth With a Mission (YWAM) began working at Smokey Mountain in 1985 and found, tragically, that families often lost young children to measles. Working with the local health authorities, an immunization clinic began in Smokey Mountain in 1986. The first Wednesday of every month became known as child immunization day at the YWAM multi-purpose center. The children received immunizations free of charge for tetanus, typhoid, pertussis (whooping cough), polio, measles, and B.C.G. (tuberculosis). Families would congregate outside the green cinder-block building as workers weighed the children and administered the shots and liquid drops. It was making a difference. In 1986, the primary health care workers there noted over 45 child deaths due to measles. In 1987, there were only 18 recorded deaths. In 1988, there were no known deaths due to measles, infections, or complications. Immunizations clearly made a difference and offered hope for the squatter community.[9]

Third, God prescribes that we house the homeless.

And bring the homeless poor
into the house. (verse 7b)

We are often hindered from ministering to the homeless by fear and by the mindset that the government has programs for this sort of thing. The promises of God (which we will see in a moment) should shatter fear. And the fact that the government is willing to help should not control our labors of love. There are structural and spontaneous ways to minister to the poor. Spontaneously we take risks and don't worry that the long-term effects may be small. Love does not calculate that way. The good Samaritan did not say, "One interrupted day will make very little difference in the problem of chronic violence in this region." He saw this one need and did something. So it is with many who see the homeless and perform their fast.

It was a bitterly cold December in Oregon. A piercing east wind sent Portlanders scurrying from warm office buildings into the shelter of their cars for the evening commute. But Les and Kathy couldn't help noticing the men and women who had no warm home waiting for them—who had no home at all. . . . Up came the deflector shields. Well, they rationalized, there were missions and those sorts of groups around that were supposed to be helping. They were the "professionals." . . . But "they" weren't getting the job done. There were still people on the streets—in full view of Les and Kathy on their way home from work—who were suffering in the sub-freezing temperature. Real people feeling real pain. They had even seen one woman with no shoes. . . . "We talked about it," Kathy recalled. "And we realized that we had three extra sleeping bags, more blankets than we needed, and a drawer full of gloves. We said, 'That's some-thing we can do,' so we did it. We went downtown and handed the stuff out" . . . Did they sell all they had? No. . . . Did they switch careers and devote full time to street peo-ple? No. . . . They simply saw a need at their "front gate," realized they could help, and responded.[10]

I am aware that what the text actually says is, "bring the homeless poor into the house." And I do believe that the more relational our care for the poor can be, the better. But it would be wooden and unchristlike to say that all care short of bringing the homeless into our own home is hypocritical. That may be what we should do in some cases, but not necessarily in all. And it is often an all-or-nothing attitude that paralyzes God's people.

And as I said, there are structural ways to do this different fasting for the poor, as well as spontaneous individual ways. The closest illustration at hand is a few blocks from my home, a min-istry called Masterworks, created by Tim Glader to help the chronically unemployed in our neighborhood to develop skills, discipline, and hope by working, for example, in simple assembly routines and meeting in Christian discipleship relationships. Tim sold his suburban heating and air-conditioning service company to start the inner-city business in 1991. He also moved into the city with his wife and kids. Our church makes the building available, and Tim does everything else. His aim is to magnify the greatness of Christ's love and power by offering almost-unemployable people secure, full-time jobs that help develop job skills while also providing the support necessary to prepare workers for the jump from welfare to self-sufficiency. This venture has been for Tim and his family no small "fast." How much easier and more secure and comfortable would have been the "feast" of plenty without having to worry with the existence of the poor.

Fourth, God prescribes that we clothe the naked.

> *When you see the naked,*
> *to cover him . . . (verse 7c)*

Fifth, he prescribes that we be sympathetic, that we feel what others feel because we have the same flesh they do.

> *And not to hide yourself*
> *from your own flesh . . . (verse 7d)*

The thought seems to be the same as Hebrews 13:3, "Remember the prisoners, as though in prison with them, and those who are ill-treated, since you yourselves also are in the body." You have the same flesh they do. So put yourself in their place and feel what they feel. One of the implications of this would seem to be that we not seal ourselves off from the places of trouble and misery. Out of sight usually means out of mind. And out of mind usually means out of heart. All of us know that one trip to the streets of Calcutta does more to change our values and priorities than many statistics. And living in the city or moving closer to the manifest needs of the poor will help keep that exposure from being a mere spasmodic experience of compassion. It is no guarantee. One can become callous anywhere. And one can do great good from afar. But the fast God prescribes includes this: don't hide from your fellow humans who are in need.

Sixth, God prescribes that we put away gestures and words that show raw contempt for other people.

> *Remove . . . the pointing of the finger*
> *and speaking wickedness . . . (verse 9)*

Literally the Hebrew means the "sending" of the finger, which may be a lot closer to our crude "giving someone the finger" than it is to merely pointing at someone. So don't gesture and don't speak in ways that show callous contempt for others. Oh, how easy it is to become fed up with the arrogant poor! The fast God prescribes for us is to renounce such an attitude and go without it. This is not easy. I used to think that living among the poor would sensitize us to the need and break our hearts. It is not that simple. It can have exactly the opposite effect. It can make you hard and caustic and jaundiced. The pleasures of "eating" such cynicism are tragically sweet. From this we must fast.

Finally, the Lord prescribes that we not just give *food*, but give *ourselves*—our souls—and not just to satisfy the stomach of the poor, but the soul of the afflicted.

> *And if you give yourself [soul] to the hungry,*
> *And satisfy the desire [soul] of the afflicted . . . (verse 10)*

The correspondence between giving our own "soul" and satisfying the "soul" of the afflicted is not evident in the English translation. But in Hebrew the same word is used in both parts of the verse. The ministry is soul to soul. One of the newer efforts of our church in the city is a partnership with an urban ministry called InnerChange. One of the great emphases that we are learning in this partnership is that ministry to the poor is not merely giving things. It is giving self. It's not just relief. It's relationship. That is an essential part of God's fasting prescription in Isaiah 58.

The All-satisfying Promises of God

Now, if we trust God, our Great Physician, enough to follow him in this prescribed seven-point fast, what will happen in our lives and in our churches? Again there are seven categories of promises—rewards from the Father who sees our fasting. They do not necessarily correspond one to one with the previous categories of prescriptions. But taken together they portray a life that many of us are longing for. O, that we would not be put off by the paradox that pouring out our lives is the way to fullness. God would give us himself, but he would have us know that he satisfies most fully when he is shared most freely.

The first promise is that the darkness in your life will become light.

> Then your light will break out like the dawn. (verse 8)
> Then your light will rise in darkness,
> And your gloom will become like midday. (verse 10)

It is one of God's many paradoxes that there is more light in the dark places of the world for those who go there to serve. And there is more darkness in the glitz of the great malls for those who go there to escape. Jesus is the Light of the world. Living near him is the brightest place in the universe. To find out where he lives, read the Gospels and follow his path.

How's the gloom factor in your life? Are *you* gloomy? Is your church gloomy? Is your Sunday school class gloomy? Is your small group under a cloud of gloom? Maybe you should stand up and say, "If there's a cast of gloom over us, maybe we should find some project for the hungry." That's what this text says. If you want the clouds to roll back, start pouring out your life for other people. Maybe you're way too ingrown as a person, or a church or a small group or a family. Maybe your family has become so self-focused, nobody ever comes over. You don't know any of your neighbors. There's no family ministry. And you wonder why there's a cloud over the family. Take this promise, and pray hard about the gloom and light factor in your life, and see whether there's a prescription here for you—not a job description to earn anything, but a doctor's prescription from a Physician who loves you and wants you free from gloom. He wants light on you, and he knows the path that leads to brightness.

Second, God promises that he will give you physical strengthening.

And your recovery will speedily spring forth. . . . (verse 8)
And [he will] give strength to your bones. . . . (verse 11)

Who knows how much weakness is in us individually and in the church corporately because we are not pouring our energy into the weakness of others? We spend our evenings watching television because we are too tired to do anything else. Perhaps. However, God promises strength not only from restful evenings alone, but from fasting from things like television in order to take a meal to the family overwhelmed with medical crises. There is a spiritual dynamic here that we do not understand until we experience it. We are made to mediate the glory of God's grace to others. For this there is strength when we think that all is spent.

Third, God will be in front of us and behind us and in the midst of us with righteousness and glory.

And your righteousness will go before you;
    The glory of the Lord will be your rear guard. (verse 8)

So God will be in front of you with righteousness and behind you with his glory. And not only that, but he will be there when you call.

Then you will call, and the Lord will answer;
    You will cry, and He will say, "Here I am." (verse 9)

Whenever you call the roll of helpers, God always says, "Here!" When we are busy doing what his Son did, namely, "becoming poor that others might become rich" (2 Corinthians 8:9), and doing it "in the power that God supplies" (1 Peter 4:11), then God moves in behind us and in front of us and surrounds us with omnipotent love and help and protection and care.

For years I have argued that prayer is meant by God to be a wartime walkie-talkie, not a domestic intercom. God intends for us to call on him to help us because we are giving our lives to spread a passion for his supremacy in all things for the joy of all peoples. Prayer is not for the enhancement of our comforts but for the advancement of Christ's kingdom. When Isaiah 58:9 says, "*Then* you will call, and the Lord will answer," "then" refers back to verse 7. When? "Then"—namely, when you join the forces of love to minister to those without food, shelter, and clothing. This is *when* the Lord will hear the wartime walkie-talkie and answer. He has very special frequencies apportioned to the territories of high-risk love.

This does not mean that you can't pray for your child to be healed from a sore throat or for your car not to break down. But it does mean that if you don't have God-exalting, kingdom-advancing reasons for those kinds of prayers, they will lead eventually to a malfunction of the walkie-talkie. Nor does it mean that there is no place for prayerful lingering with God in the communion of praise and fellowship. But it does mean that the consummation of joy in communion with God is a shared joy. And praise that is not tending toward the inclusion of others will spoil.

Fourth, God promises to guide us continually.

> *And the Lord will continually*
> *guide you. (verse 11)*

Oh, what a precious promise this is for us in the perplexities of life and ministry! I wonder how much confusion and uncertainty in our lives comes from the neglect of ministry to the poor? It seems the Lord gives his most intimate guidance to those bent on giving themselves to the needs of others—especially the poor. The guidance of God is not meant for the bright paths of the garden of ease, but for the dark places of pain where we have few answers and paths have never been cut. How many times in the pastoral ministry have I been called to come to a crisis, and as I go I say, "Lord, I don't know what the solution is here. Help me. Please grant me your guidance. Bring to my mind what would be most helpful." Again and again he has answered. Make yourself available, even for situations of need beyond your ability, and "the Lord will continually guide you."

Fifth, he will satisfy your soul.

> *And [he will] satisfy your desire* [your soul]
> *in scorched places. (verse 11)*

Our souls are meant to be satisfied in God. But we have learned again and again that this satisfaction in God comes to consummation when we extend our satisfaction in him to others. Pouring ourselves out for the poor is the path of deepest satisfaction. And note that this will come "in scorched places." In other words, in the service of others, your soul will become less and less dependent on external circumstances for satisfaction. More and more you will be able to say with the psalmist in Psalm 73:25-26:

> Whom have I in heaven but Thee?
>   And besides Thee, I desire nothing on earth.
> My flesh and my heart may fail,
>   But God is the strength of my heart and my portion forever.

Sixth, God will make you a watered garden with springs that do not fail.

> And you will be like a watered garden,
>   And like a spring of water whose waters do not fail. (verse 11)

This was the verse that wakened Bill Leslie to the preciousness of the "fast" of Isaiah 58. He, along with many pastors, was going through a dry season. But there in one verse was what we all need and want—both being watered and the power to water others: "a watered garden" and "a spring of water." It is a paradoxical spiritual principle in Scripture: as you pour yourself out, you become full. As you give away, you get more.

But there is an assumption that the well has been dug and is being kept unclogged. We can only stay green and useful for others if there is, as it were, a spring in our soul. And what is that? This promise comes to its fulfillment in the New Testament through what Jesus revealed in John 7:38, "He who believes in Me, as the Scripture said, 'From his innermost being shall flow rivers of living water' [a spring of waters that does not fail]. But this He spoke of the Spirit, whom those who believed in Him were to receive." In other words, trusting in Jesus for all we need is the opening of the spring of the Spirit's power. And he bestirs himself most fully when, by faith, we spend ourselves in the path of love for the sake of the perishing and the poor.

Finally, if we give ourselves to the poor, God will restore the ruins of his city—and his people.

> *And those from among you will rebuild the ancient ruins;*
> *You will raise up the age-old foundations;*
> *And you will be called the repairer of the breach,*
> *The restorer of the streets in which to dwell.* (verse 12)

How many ruined things may be repaired by the fasting of God's people for the sake of the poor! Who knows what miseries, what dysfunctions, what breaches, what afflictions and oppressions may be healed and restored by the beautiful fasting of Isaiah 58! Ours is not to predict what the city or the church or the family or society might look like. Ours is to trust and obey.

So let us trust the Great Physician, the Lord, our healer. Let us accept the fast that he has prescribed for us. It will mean light and healing and guidance and refreshment and restoration and resourcefulness—and all of this with God himself before us, and behind us, and in the midst of us. And since it is by our good deeds that people will see our light and give glory to our Father in heaven (Matthew 5:16), then this fast too will spread the gospel of the kingdom and hasten the day of the Lord. If we are truly hungry for all the fullness of God, here is a fasting that will fill.

Then I proclaimed a fast there at the river of Ahava,
that we might humble ourselves before our God
to seek from Him a safe journey for us, our little ones,
and all our possessions.

—EZRA 8:21

Judge not the Lord by feeble sense,
But trust him for his grace,
Behind a frowning providence
He hides a smiling face.

His purposes will ripen fast,
Unfolding ev'ry hour;
The bud may have a bitter taste,
But sweet will be the flower.

—WILLIAM COWPER
"God Moves in a Mysterious Way"[1]

7

FASTING FOR THE LITTLE ONES

Abortion and the Sovereignty of God Over False Worldviews

Our hunger for God is too small. This is true not only because our capacities to desire are atrophied—like a muscle that lifts only feathers—but also because our capacity to see the Desirable is untrained on the telescope of God's Word.

On What Do We Exercise the Muscle of Desire?

We are meant to desire the Great with great desire.

> *Whom have I in heaven but Thee? And besides Thee, I desire nothing on earth. My flesh and my heart may fail, but God is the strength of my heart and my portion forever.*
> *—Psalm 73:25-26*

> *As the deer pants for the water brooks, So my soul pants for Thee, O God. My soul thirsts for God, for the living God.*
> *—Psalm 42:1-2*

*O God, Thou art my God; I shall seek Thee earnestly; My
soul thirsts for Thee, my flesh yearns for Thee, in a dry and
weary land where there is no water.*

—*Psalm 63:1*

*I count all things to be loss in view of the surpassing value
of knowing Christ Jesus my Lord, for whom I have suffered
the loss of all things, and count them but rubbish in order
that I may gain Christ.*

—*Philippians 3:8*

But we flex our desires for small things rather than for God.
And so the very potential for desire diminishes.

How Large Are the Tiny Stars?

And we do not put our eye often to the telescope of God's Word
where the tiny twinklings of God in our cluttered night sky are
revealed as unspeakably great wonders. How often do we pray
with the psalmist, "Open my eyes, that I may behold wonderful
things from Thy law" (Psalm 119:18)? And if we do not see him
in his greatness, we will not desire him in his fullness.

Beholding the glory of God is not only a private experience
on a mountain as he passes by. It is also a public experience as he
multiplies plagues in the land of Egypt, and divides the Red Sea,
and swallows the family of Korah into the earth, and turns water
into wine, and raises the dead, and causes selfish men to lay down
their lives for the sake of love, and turns the hearts of kings toward
the cause of Truth. There is a hunger for God that goes beyond
the desire for private experience. It longs for the public display of
his glory in the world. It longs for the great dishonors against our
God to be set right. It is not content to hope for private revelations of his saving help, as precious as they are. It yearns for the
open triumph of his hand in the establishment of God-exalting

truth and righteousness—in universities and courts of law and advertising agencies and political debates and all the media of television and radio and newspapers and magazines and movies and the Internet. It is driven by a passion for the supremacy of God in all things for the joy of all peoples.

Fasting for the Public Glory of God

If fasting is an exclamation point after the sentence of the heart, "O God, show us your glory!" then fasting is not merely a private matter either. It has to do with the public, historical, cultural, global demonstrations of the glory of God that our hearts desire. That is what this chapter is about. Taking abortion as one manifestation of a great godlessness in our culture, how shall we then live and pray and fast?

Francis Schaeffer's Vindication

Francis Schaeffer died on May 5, 1984. Thirteen years later *Christianity Today* featured his picture on the front of the magazine over the caption, "Our Saint Francis." In Michael Hamilton's lead essay we read the tribute that in the last twenty years of his life

> perhaps no intellectual save C.S. Lewis affected the thinking of evangelicals more profoundly; perhaps no leader of the period save Billy Graham left a deeper stamp on the movement [of American evangelicalism] as a whole. Together the Schaeffers gave currency to the idea of intentional Christian community, prodded evangelicals out of their cultural ghetto, inspired an army of evangelicals to become serious scholars, encouraged women who chose roles as mothers and homemakers, mentored the leaders of the New

Christian Right, and solidified popular evangelical opposition to abortion.[2]

Almost twenty years have passed since Schaeffer, together with C. Everett Koop, launched his missile against abortion, *Whatever Happened to the Human Race?* (1979)—a book, a film series, and a speaking tour. The amazing thing today at the end of the twentieth century is how up-to-date it still sounds, and how prophetic it has proved to be. Michael Hamilton acknowledges in his 1997 article that "some critics have recently allowed that [Schaeffer's] big picture has proven durable. . . . In particular, he appears to have been prescient on the issue of human life."[3]

When I turn back to Schaeffer's two-decades-old words, they have that prophetic ring of durability and truth.

> In the flood of the loss of humanness in our age—including the flow from abortion-on-demand to infanticide and on to euthanasia—the only thing that can stem this tide is the certainty of the absolute uniqueness and value of people. And the only thing which gives us that is the knowledge that people are made in the image of God. We have no other final protection. And the only way we know that people are made in the image of God is through the Bible and the incarnation of Christ, which we know from the Bible.
>
> If people are not made in the image of God, the pessimistic, realistic humanist is right: the human race is an abnormal wart on the smooth face of a silent and meaningless universe. In this setting, abortion, infanticide, and euthanasia (including the killing of mentally deranged criminals, the severely handicapped, or the elderly who are an economic burden) are completely logical. . . . Without the Bible and without the revelation in Christ (which is only told to us in the Bible) there is nothing to stand between us and our children and the eventual acceptance of the monstrous inhumanities of the age.[4]

Michael Hamilton comments that "Schaeffer's bleak vision is now daily news."

"Cadaver Jack" Kevorkian has already killed more people than Ted Bundy, but the state of Michigan cannot muster the political will to stop him. A federal court has forbidden the state of Washington to pass laws preventing doctors from killing their patients, while the University of Washington is permitted to scavenge and sell the body parts of thousands of aborted children every year.[5]

The Most Permissive Abortion Democracy in the World

It would not surprise Francis Schaeffer that America has become the most permissive of all democratic societies in the modern world when it comes to abortion.

Mary Ann Glendon of Harvard Law School is *the* authority on abortion law in the Western world. She notes that, of all democratic societies, the U.S. is far and away the most permissive on abortion. . . . She observes, the now-united Germany adopted a new abortion law providing significant protections for the unborn. As is the case in every democracy except the U.S., the law was adopted through legislative politics. But the Supreme Court has in effect declared that the American people, once thought to be the teachers of the world in the ways of democracy, are peculiarly unfitted for self-governance.[6]

This strange power of the Supreme Court symbolizes how intractable the American position seems to be. Its logic is that 1.6 million lives a year are

the price that must be paid in order not to interfere with lifestyles that presuppose abortion on demand. That is the judgment imposed by judicial fiat on a society in which 75 percent of the people say that abortions should not be allowed for the reasons that 95 percent of abortions are in fact performed.[7]

There is a kind of desperation that begins to grip a people ruled not by legislators, but by judges who declare the Constitution to mean what they say it means. This desperation leads to talk of desperate measures. We have already had killings. This too would not have surprised Francis Schaeffer, who "defined abortion as the hinge issue for American society, called Christians to civil disobedience, and even broached the idea of resisting the government by force."[8] He concluded one of his last books, *A Christian Manifesto*, in 1981, with the words, "If there is no final place for civil disobedience, then the government has been made autonomous, and as such, it has been put in the place of the Living God."[9]

The Legitimacy of the American Regime?

Again in fulfillment of Schaeffer's warnings there have been stunning recent public discussions of the possible illegitimacy of the present American regime. In 1996 and 1997, a symposium including, among others, William Bennett, Robert Bork, Charles Colson, James Dobson, and Richard John Neuhaus addressed this issue. "The question here explored, in full awareness of its far-reaching consequences, is whether we have reached or are reaching the point where conscientious citizens can no longer give moral assent to the existing regime."[10]

There is no endorsement here of killing abortionists. But there is the sober judgment that "A civilization cannot tolerate private executions, as a civilization cannot long survive the license to kill unwanted human beings."[11] How long, is the question. Richard Neuhaus observes that "the destructive effects of anomie and anger are already evident as a result of law divorced from constitutional text, moral argument, and democratic process. The ever-fragile bonds of civility are unraveled as politics becomes, to paraphrase Clausewitz, war pursued by other means. Lawless law is an invitation to lawlessness."[12]

What Abortion Teaches a Nation

Meanwhile, the abortion license eats away at one precious thing after another. The children are the first to go. The women next, with the guilt and the heartbreak and the physical harm and the manifold effects of post-abortion syndrome.[13] Then come the fathers with some remorse and anger and huge amounts of "irresponsibility and predatory male sexual behavior" encouraged by the assumption that there is a simple solution to any unwanted pregnancy. Then comes the erosion of the moral landscape that depends so much on virtues and values and commitments that go beyond mere autonomous individual liberties.

In February 1995, before the President of the United States at the National Prayer Breakfast, Mother Teresa spoke with courage and directness concerning this erosive effect of abortion.

> I feel that the greatest destroyer of peace today is abortion, because it is a war against the child—a direct killing of the innocent child—murder by the mother herself. And if we accept that a mother can kill even her own child, how can we tell other people not to kill one another? . . .
>
> By abortion, the mother does not learn to love, but kills even her own child to solve her problems. And by abortion, the father is told that he does not have to take any responsibility at all for the child he has brought into the world. That father is likely to put other women into the same trou-

ble. So abortion just leads to more abortion. Any country that accepts abortion is not teaching the people to love, but to use any violence to get what they want. That is why the greatest destroyer of love and peace is abortion.[14]

This is what Francis Schaeffer meant when he said, "Compassion . . . is being undermined. And it is not only the babies who are being killed; it is humanness which the humanist worldview is beating to death."[15]

On Not Seeing Things in Bits and Pieces

Here is where Francis Schaeffer is at his best—at the level of worldviews. And this is surely the level at which the great battles of the universe are fought. Schaeffer said that "the basic problem of the Christians in this country in the last eighty years or so . . . is that they have seen things in bits and pieces instead of totals."[16] He means that the worldviews behind the bits and pieces—like abortion—have not been understood and resisted. The name he gives the worldview that sustains, while it can, the modern West, including abortion, is "the material-energy, chance view of final reality."

We must try to roll back the results of the total worldview which considers material-energy, shaped by chance, as the final reality. We must realize that this view will with inevitable certainty always bring forth results which are not only relativistic, and not only wrong, but which will be inhuman, not only for other people, but for our children and grandchildren, and our spiritual children. It will always bring forth what is inhuman, for with its false view of total reality it not only does not have a basis for the uniqueness and dignity of the individual person, but it is totally ignorant as to what, and who Man is.[17]

God, not material-energy is the final reality. And he, not chance, shapes all things. The restoration of this foundation—the supremacy of God in all things—is the great challenge of the western world. A worldview built on matter and chance "leaves no room for meaning, purpose, or values in the universe and gives no base for law. . . . Its control of the consensus has become overwhelmingly dominant in about the last forty years."[18]

A Worldview War on Abortion

This is the context for our opposition to abortion. So Schaeffer recommends not just that we resist the "bits and pieces" but the whole worldview in the way we pray and struggle and work. "Certainly every Christian ought to be praying and working to nullify the abominable abortion law. But as we work and pray, we should have in mind not only this important issue as though it stood alone. Rather, we should be struggling and praying that this whole other total entity—the material-energy, chance worldview—can be rolled back with all its results across all of life."[19]

The most compelling pro-life efforts today grasp this goal. David Reardon's vision is one example that connects even explicitly with Schaeffer's worldview approach. Reardon, a biomedical ethicist, echoes Schaeffer's concern in his specific strategy:

> The political goal of making abortion illegal has always been a truncate vision. Our real desire has always been to create a culture where abortion is not just illegal, but is *unthinkable*. In such a culture, the physical, psychological, and spiritual dangers of abortion will be common knowledge. In such a culture, commitment, compassion, and a

sense of duty to aid and protect both mother and the child will be universal.[20]

The key word is "unthinkable." And it was Schaeffer, seventeen years earlier, who said, "There is a 'thinkable' and an 'unthinkable' in every era."[21] And it is the underlying worldview that governs what is thinkable and unthinkable. Therefore, Reardon and Schaeffer, and most thoughtful people today, realize that the battle over abortion is a much deeper battle for the soul of the culture and its worldview.[22]

The Place of Prayer and Fasting

How then shall we resist and reform? In the last years of his life Schaeffer was increasingly oriented on the political arena and increasingly disenchanted with the narrow piety of evangelicalism—the "*majority* of the Silent Majority" who had "two bankrupt values—personal peace and affluence."[23] His emphasis was a prophetic and timely call.

But I wonder if many of the young scholars and activists (now in their forties and fifties!) whom he inspired need to hear a balancing word about the power of prayer and fasting, not as an alternative to thinking and acting, but as a radical foundation that says, "The victory belongs to the Lord, even if the horse (of scholarship and politics) is made ready for the day of battle" (see Proverbs 21:31). Listen to the books crying out for evangelical renewal and reformation in the life of the mind, the restoration of Truth in the place of technique, the recovery of church social compassion from government powerlessness, the taking of moral high ground in the environmental cause, and many other causes. Is there a sense in each of these that the root issues are so intractable to human suasion that the call for fasting and prayer would not only be fitting but desperately needed? I am commending such a call.

Fasting and Praying for Worldview Breakthroughs

This was not Schaeffer's main call at the end of his life, and for some today it is not part of their horizon—that fasting and prayer might bring the breakthroughs they write about and work for so passionately. Schaeffer did say, "Every Christian ought to be praying and working to nullify the abominable abortion law. . . . We should be struggling and praying that this whole other total entity—the material-energy, chance worldview—can be rolled back."[24] I wonder if the scholars and activists take even that to heart. I confess that my own praying for worldview breakthroughs is not what it should be. Oh, how easily I settle into a resigned and fatalistic frame of mind when it comes to secular mindsets, and defective theologies, and institutional corruption, and philosophical falsehood, and pervasive cultural biases.

But this is not the time for resignation or fatalism. It is the time for radical prayer and fasting to the end that all our thinking and all our preaching and all our writing and all our social action and missions will have the aroma of God on it and will carry a transforming thrust far beyond anything mere man could do. Then might it be said, beyond all expectation and human possibility, "Five of you will chase a hundred, and a hundred of you will chase ten thousand, and your enemies will fall before you" (Leviticus 26:8).

Avoiding a Siege Mentality in Babylon

Where shall we get the confidence and the encouragement to fast and pray for such sweeping worldview concerns?

I suggest that we consider the biblical story of Ezra, especially Ezra 8:21-23. Let me give you some faith-building background to this text so you hear it with all the force Ezra gives it, and with all its relevance for our worldview concerns.

Israel had been taken into Babylonian exile. They had been there for decades. Now the time had come, in God's reckoning, for their restoration. But how could this happen? They were a tiny, obscure ethnic minority in the massive Persian empire. The answer is that God rules empires. And when it is his time for his people to move, he moves empires. That's the point of the first eight chapters of this book of Ezra. And it is massively hope-giving for the people of God every time we slip back into a mentality of siege.

Consider, first, Ezra 1:1-2.

> Now in the first year of Cyrus king of Persia, in order to fulfill the word of the Lord by the mouth of Jeremiah, the Lord stirred up the spirit of Cyrus king of Persia, so that he sent a proclamation throughout all his kingdom, and also put it in writing, saying, "Thus says Cyrus king of Persia, 'The Lord, the God of heaven, has given me all the kingdoms of the earth, and He has appointed me to build Him a house in Jerusalem, which is in Judah.'"

Do not miss the sovereign rule of God over the mind and will of Cyrus, the most powerful king in the world. God had prophesied by Jeremiah that the people would come back to their own land. "For thus says the LORD, 'When seventy years have been completed for Babylon, I will visit you and fulfill My good word to you, to bring you back to this place'" (Jeremiah 29:10). God never leaves his prophesies dangling uncertainly in the will of man. He does not merely predict; he acts to fulfill the predictions he makes. This is why his predictions are as sure as he is powerful.

So it says in Ezra 1:1, "He stirred up the spirit of Cyrus."

Cyrus did not merely experience inexplicably the fulfillment of a prophecy; he experienced God himself working sovereignly to fulfill that prophecy. There's the answer. When God is ready to do a great thing in the world, he can do it—whether it is through a Persian king, or a prophet, or a scholarly book, or a Christian pro-life worker. The key is God's absolute sovereignty over the empires of the world and over the minds and wills of kings and scholars and politicians and university presidents.

Even the Setbacks Are Meant for Greater Benefit

Here is what happens. A first wave of refugees return to Israel from Babylon—over 42,000 of them. They start building the temple. But their enemies in Judah oppose them and write to the new emperor, Artaxerxes, telling him that a rebellious city is being rebuilt (4:12). So Artaxerxes halts the work on the temple, and it looks like God's plans are frustrated. This is often the way things go—a great movement in the right direction in the church or in a city or in the culture as a whole, and then a setback. This often sets to moaning pessimists who have small views of God. But this story is meant to keep us hoping.

God had a different and better plan that was not just in spite of the opposition and setback, but that included it. O, let us learn that the lean years of trouble are preparations for God's blessing! Sooner or later he turns it all for good. He is God. In this case here is how he does it. According to Ezra 5:1, God sends two prophets, Haggai and Zechariah, who inspire the people to begin building again.

> *"But now take courage, Zerubbabel" declares the LORD,*
> *"take courage also, Joshua son of Jehozadak, the high priest,*
> *and all you people of the land, take courage," declares the*
> *LORD, "and work; for I am with you," says the LORD of*

*hosts. . . . "The silver is Mine, and the gold is Mine," declares
the LORD of hosts. "The latter glory of this house will be
greater than the former," says the LORD of hosts.*
                                                    —Haggai 2:4, 8-9

But, as is often the case, a new resurgence of energy and
progress unleashes new opposition. So it is here: the enemies try
the same tactic as before. This time they write a letter to Darius,
the new emperor, in the hopes of bringing the work in
Jerusalem to a halt. But this time it backfires, and we get to see
why God had allowed the building to cease temporarily in the
first place.

Darius does some research before responding to the enemies of Israel. He searches the archives and finds the original
decree from Cyrus authorizing the building of the temple. So in
Ezra 6:7-8 he writes back the stunning news—beyond anything
the bedraggled Israelites could ask or think. Darius says to the
enemies in Judah,

> *Leave this work on the house of God alone; let the gover-
> nor of the Jews and the elders of the Jews rebuild this house
> of God on its site. Moreover, I issue a decree concerning
> what you are to do for these elders of Judah in the rebuild-
> ing of this house of God:* the full cost is to be paid to these
> people from the royal treasury *out of the taxes of the
> provinces beyond the River, and that without delay.*

What a remarkable reversal! What a great God! The Jews
thought the enemies had triumphed. But God was simply working history so that the enemies would not only *permit* the building of the temple but *pay* for it too! Ezra 6:22 states the great fact
plainly: "*The Lord had turned the heart of the king of Assyria
toward them* to encourage them in the work of the house of God,
the God of Israel." God rules the hearts of kings and emperors

and presidents and scientists and scholars and judges and governors and mayors. This is the great foundation for fasting and prayer for worldview concerns—God can convert people, and God can shape their thinking even if they are not converted. O, the lessons here for us in our struggle to bring truth to bear on the church and the culture.

> *Judge not the Lord by feeble sense,*
> *But trust him for his grace,*
> *Behind a frowning providence*
> *He hides a smiling face.*[25]

O, the lessons here for us! Name your discouraging setback—personal, political, scholarly, ecclesiastical, cultural, global. Dare any Christian say that God is not in this for the good of his people and the glory of his name? Not if our God is the God of Ezra! Do you think these setbacks are not without some great purpose of righteousness bigger and more stunning than any of us can imagine?

The King's Heart Is a Stream of Water in the Hand of God

Then Ezra comes into the picture with a flashback to the reign of Artaxerxes. The king sends Ezra with a company of people back to Jerusalem. According to Ezra 7:6 the king gives him everything he wants for the journey. Now why would the very king who stopped the building of the temple do that? Ezra gives the answer in his prayer in 7:27. "Blessed be the Lord, the God of our fathers, *who has put such a thing as this in the king's heart.*" God did it. God put it in his heart.

He did it to Cyrus (1:1); he did it to Darius (6:22); and he did it to Artaxerxes (7:27). "The king's heart is like channels of water in the hand of the LORD; He turns it wherever He wishes"

(Proverbs 21:1). God is ruling the world. He is ruling history. "Oh, the depth of the riches both of the wisdom and knowledge of God! How unsearchable are His judgments and unfathomable His ways!" (Romans 11:33). We cannot understand the infinite wisdom of his ways. Ours is to trust and obey and pray—and as we shall see, to fast.

Fasting Before a World-sovereign God

Which brings us to what Ezra did as he left captivity on his way to Jerusalem. He refused an army escort so that he could testify to Artaxerxes about the power and faithfulness of God in protecting his company of people. Instead of the king's help he sought God's help, and he sought it *with fasting*. Ezra 8:21-23 records:

> *Then* I proclaimed a fast *there at the river of Ahava, that we might humble ourselves before our God to seek from Him a safe journey for us,* our little ones [here is the connection with saving little ones from abortion] *and all our possessions. For I was ashamed to request from the king troops and horsemen to protect us from the enemy on the way, because we had said to the king, "The hand of our God is favorably disposed to all those who seek Him, but His power and His anger are against all those who forsake Him." So we fasted and sought our God concerning this matter, and He listened to our entreaty.*

In verse 21, fasting is an expression of humility—that is, our sense of desperate, utter dependence on God for what we need. "I proclaimed *a fast* there at the river of Ahava, that we might *humble ourselves*." And if anything is plain from Francis Schaeffer's analysis of the foundations of abortion, it is that the humanist worldview pervading American culture is so intractable that we are utterly dependent on God to resist and reform. Faithful reasoning, persuasive writing, social activism and political engagement all have their place. But unless the sovereign God moves on darkened minds (like he did on Cyrus and Darius and Artaxerxes), the very best reasoning and action will be taken captive and turned upside down.

But fasting, for Ezra, was not only an expression of humility and desperation; it was an expression of desiring God with life-and-death seriousness. "So we fasted and sought our God." Fasting comes in alongside prayer with all its hunger for God and says, "We are not able in ourselves to win this battle. We are not able to change hearts or minds. We are not able to change worldviews and transform culture and save 1.6 million children. We are not able to reform the judiciary or embolden the legislature or mobilize the slumbering population. We are not able to heal the endless wounds of godless ideologies and their bloody deeds. But, O God, you are able! And we turn from reliance on ourselves to you. And we cry out to you and plead that for the sake of your name, and for the sake of your glory, and for the advancement of your saving purpose in the world, and for the demonstration of your wisdom and your power and your authority over all things, and for the sway of your Truth and the relief of the poor and the helpless, act, O God. This much we hunger for the revelation of your power. With all our thinking and all our writing and all our doing, we pray and we fast. Come. Manifest your glory."

The merciful result of fasting and prayer is mentioned at the end of Ezra 8:23: "He listened to our entreaty." The children were spared. The heart of the king was swayed. The enemies were turned away. This is an astonishing thing—that a God who sways the minds of kings should ordain that he be swayed by the weak to send his sovereign power on their behalf.

"Doing Business" Until He Comes

I appeal to you to seek the Lord with me concerning the place of fasting and prayer in breaking through the darkened mind that engulfs the modern world, in regard to abortion and a hundred other ills. This is not a call for a collective tantrum that screams at the bad people, "Give me back my country." It is a call to aliens and exiles in the earth, whose citizenship is in heaven and who await the appearance of their King, to "do business" until he comes (Luke 19:13). And the great business of the Christian is to "do all to the glory of God" (1 Corinthians 10:31), and to pray that God's name be hallowed and his kingdom come and his will be done in the earth (Matthew 6:9-10). And to yearn and work and pray and fast not only for the final revelation of the Son of Man, but in the meantime, for the demonstration of his Spirit and power in the reaching of every people, and the rescuing of the perishing, and the purifying of the church, and the putting right of as many wrongs as God will grant.

It is true that the biblical balance of labor among such great tasks is not an easy discovery. But that too may be a fruit of faithful fasting. May the Lord grant that the greatness of our calling not paralyze our desires. But may our hunger for private and public displays of the glory of our great God find release in fasting and prayer and every good work.

Blessed are you who hunger now,
for you shall be satisfied.

—LUKE 6:21

Or who has first given to Him
that it might be paid back to Him again?
For from Him and through Him and to Him are all things.
To Him be the glory forever. Amen.

—ROMANS 11:35-36

God has been pleased to constitute prayer to be
antecedent to the bestowment of mercy; and he is
pleased to bestow mercy in consequence of prayer, as
though he were prevailed on by prayer. When the people of God are stirred up to prayer, it is the effect of
his intention to show mercy; therefore he pours out
the spirit of grace and supplication.

—JONATHAN EDWARDS
"The Most High a Prayer-Hearing God"[1]

CONCLUSION

_____

Why Does God
Reward Fasting?

One crucial question remains: Why does God respond to fasting? Why does he reward us when we fast? That he does is strewn across the pages of the Bible and history. And Jesus promised he would: "Your Father who sees [your fasting] in secret will reward you" (Matthew 6:18, RSV). The question is urgent because a wrong answer can dishonor God and do us great harm.

An Answer That Dishonors God and Does Us Harm

For example, suppose we said that fasting gets rewards from God because it earns them by showing the merit of the one who fasts. That would dishonor God by turning his free grace into a business transaction. It would imply that fasting springs ultimately from our own will, and that this self-created discipline is then offered to God for recompense. This is a great dishonor to God because it claims for us what belongs only to God, namely, the ultimate initiative of prayer and fasting. In this way we put ourselves in the place of God and nullify the freedom of his grace.

This also does us great harm. If we choose to relate to God this way, in the end we will not be the beneficiaries of grace, but only of retributive justice. That will mean that we get from God what we deserve, rather than the "free gift" of eternal life (Romans 6:23). To use the terms of the apostle Paul, this way of viewing God's response to fasting turns it into "works." We see this in Romans 4:4—"Now to the one who *works*, his wage is not reckoned as a favor, but as what is due." Translated literally: "To the one who works, the reward is not reckoned according to grace, but according to debt." If we say God rewards fasting by paying "wages" or settling "debts" with those who have earned or merited his reward by fasting, then we act as though "the reward is not reckoned according to grace." And that is a fatal way to relate to God. For the only alternative to free grace is condemnation.

God does not save us "by grace . . . through faith" (Ephesians 2:8) and then reward our fasting "by justice . . . through works." The reward of justification and every subsequent reward come to us on the same grounds and by the same means: on the ground of God's work in Christ, namely, his atoning death (Romans 3:24), and by the means of God's work in us, namely, our life-changing faith (Ephesians 2:8; Galatians 5:6). The attempt to merit or earn anything from God is evil and fatal before and after our conversion. An act that nullifies grace is evil and fatal whenever you do it.

Therefore, a wrong answer to the question of why God rewards fasting can dishonor God and do us great harm. It is extremely important that we answer the question correctly. God's glory and our good are at stake.

Fasting Is "from Him and Through Him and to Him"

God does not respond to fasting because it presents him with new knowledge about our faith or our devotion. He knows our hearts better than we know them ourselves. In fact, our newborn heart of faith is the handiwork of God himself. He knows us because he knows his own work. "We are his workmanship, created in Christ Jesus" (Ephesians 2:10). And he not only created us as new creatures of faith, but is still "working in us that which is pleasing in His sight" (Hebrews 13:21). It is our duty and delight to choose obedience hour by hour, but we must never forget that "it is God who is at work in [us], both to will and to work for His good pleasure" (Philippians 2:13).

The most fundamental reason why fasting cannot earn anything from God is that it is a gift of God. It is something that God is "working in us." You can't expect God to pay for what is already his. This is what Paul meant when he said in Romans 11:35-36, "Who has first given to [God] that it might be paid back to him again? For from Him and through Him and to Him are all things. To Him be the glory forever. Amen." That includes fasting. It is from him and through him and to him. It is not first offered to God that we might be paid back because of it. It is first given by God that we might benefit from it and that he might be glorified through it.

The Ultimate Origin of Sacrifice

When King Solomon saw his people sacrificing their riches to build the temple, in the same way that one might sacrifice food in fasting, he was not puffed up with the self-wrought virtue of his people; he was humbled that God had given such a grace of generosity. He said, "Who am I and who are my people that we should be able to offer as generously as this? For all things come from Thee, and from Thy hand we have given Thee" (1 Chronicles 29:14). This is the way we should speak of fasting. There is no ground of boasting here. Who am I that I should be able to fast? Nobody. There is nothing in me that would choose this for your glory apart from your transforming grace. And when Solomon looked to the future and pondered whether this heart of sacrifice would continue, he prayed, "O LORD . . . preserve this forever in the intentions of the heart of Thy people, and direct their heart to Thee" (1 Chronicles 29:18). And so we should pray about our own fasting and the fasting of the Christian church: O Lord, keep alive the intentions to fast that you have created, and direct the hearts of your people ever to you as the source of all their joy.

Reward Is for Helplessness and Hope in God

Well, if God does not reward fasting because *we* create it and offer it to him to get a recompense, why does he reward it? If, in fact, God himself is the Creator and Sustainer of fasting, why is it that he has appointed this act as an occasion of his reward? The answer is that God is committed to rewarding those acts of the human heart that signify human helplessness and hope in God. Over and over again in Scripture God promises to come to the aid of those who stop depending on themselves and seek God as their treasure and help.

"Ho! Every one who thirsts, come to the waters; and you who have no money come, buy and eat. Come, buy wine and milk without money and without cost. . . . Listen carefully to Me, and eat what is good, and delight yourself in abundance. Incline your ear and come to Me. Listen, that you may live" (Isaiah 55:1-3). God promises water and wine and milk and life that money cannot buy precisely to those who have no money, but only thirst, if they will turn away from what money can buy and come to him. "I will give to the one who thirsts from the spring of the water of life without cost. . . . Let the one who is thirsty come; let the one who wishes take the water of life without cost" (Revelation 21:6; 22:17). The reward of life comes not to those who can buy it or work for it. It is "without cost." It is free. The "price" is thirst that turns from the broken cisterns of the world to the inexhaustible fountain in God.

It is the "poor in spirit" who will be rewarded with the kingdom of heaven (Matthew 5:3). It is those who "wait for the Lord" for whom he works (Isaiah 64:4). It is those who "trust in God," and not their horses or chariots, who triumph by his power (1 Chronicles 5:20; 2 Chronicles 13:18; Psalm 20:7). It is those who "delight in the Lord" and trust in him who get the desires of their heart (Psalm 37:4-5). The sacrifices acceptable to God are a broken spirit and a contrite heart; these empty things he will reward (Psalm 51:17). The one who serves God not in his own strength but "by the strength which God supplies" will be rewarded by the Lord (1 Peter 4:11).

God's Ultimate Commitment: His Glory

God rewards those acts of the human heart that signify human helplessness and hope in God. The reason for this is that these acts call attention to God's glory. First Peter 4:11 makes this plain: "whoever serves, let him do so as by the strength which God supplies; so that in all things God may be glorified through Jesus Christ, to whom belongs the glory and dominion forever and ever. Amen." Be sure to see the logic of the verse: if you serve not in your own strength, but in the strength that God supplies, then God gets the glory. The giver gets the glory.

God is committed to doing everything for his glory. This too is shown throughout the Scriptures, as Jonathan Edwards has demonstrated so powerfully in his essay entitled *Dissertation Concerning the End for which God Created the World.* "It appears that all that is ever spoken of in the Scripture as an ultimate end of God's works is included in that one phrase, 'the glory of God.'"[2] God elects his people before the foundation of the world for his glory (Ephesians 1:6). He creates humankind for his glory (Isaiah 43:7). He chooses Israel for his glory (Isaiah 49:3). He delivers them from Egypt for his glory (Psalm 106:7-8). He restores them after exile for his glory (Isaiah 48:9-11). He sends his Son to confirm his trustworthiness and so the Gentiles will glorify him for his mercy (Roman 15:8-9). He puts his Son to death to display the glory of his vindicated righteousness (Romans 3:25-26). He sends the Holy Spirit to glorify his Son (John 16:14). He commands his people to do all things for his glory (1 Corinthians 10:31). He will send his Son a second time to receive the glory due him (2 Thessalonians 1:9-10). And in the end he will fill the earth with the knowledge of his glory (Habakkuk 2:14).

God's ultimate aim in all that he does is that his glory might be displayed for the appreciation of those who embrace it, and the desolation of those who don't. Therefore he rewards acts that confess human helplessness and that express hope in God, because these acts call attention to his glory.

An Offering of Emptiness to Show Where Fullness Can Be Found

Prayer is explicitly appointed for this purpose: "Whatever you ask in My name, that will I do, *that the Father may be glorified in the Son*" (John 14:13). God responds to prayer because when we look away from ourselves to Christ as our only hope, that gives the Father an occasion to magnify the glory of his grace in the all-providing work of his Son.

Similarly, fasting is peculiarly suited to glorify God in this way. It is fundamentally an offering of emptiness to God in hope. It is a sacrifice of need and hunger. It says, by its very nature, "Father, I am empty, but you are full. I am hungry, but you are the Bread of Heaven. I am thirsty, but you are the Fountain of Life. I am weak, but you are strong. I am poor, but you are rich. I am foolish, but you are wise. I am broken, but you are whole. I am dying, but your steadfast love is better than life (Psalm 63:3)."

When God sees this confession of need and this expression of trust, he acts, because the glory of his all-sufficient grace is at stake. The final answer is that God rewards fasting because fasting expresses the cry of the heart that nothing on the earth can satisfy our souls besides God. God must reward this cry because God is most glorified in us when we are most satisfied in him.

Remember those who led you,
who spoke the word of God to you;
and considering the result of their conduct,
imitate their faith.

—HEBREWS 13:7

Some, under the pretence of being taught of the Spirit of God, refuse to be instructed by books or by living men. This is no honoring of the Spirit of God. It is disrespect to Him, for if He gives to some of His servants more light than to others—and it is clear He does—then they are bound to give that light to others, and to use it for the good of the church. But if the other part of the church refuse to receive that light, to what end did the Spirit of God give it? This would imply that there is a mistake somewhere in the economy of God's gifts and graces, which is managed by the Holy Spirit.

—CHARLES SPURGEON
Words of Counsel for Christian Workers[1]

APPENDIX

Quotes and
Experiences

These quotes and experiences are a sampling from the reading I have done in preparation for this book. I include them here for inspiration and instruction, but with no claim to agree with all that is said. The sources are given so that the reader can follow up in the context. Sometimes just a passing comment can have as much impact on us as a whole chapter or a book. It may be that God would use one of these brief statements to awaken in someone *A Hunger for God*.

IGNATIUS
(Bishop of Antioch at the end of the first century)

Devote thyself to fasting and prayer, but not beyond measure, lest thou destroy thyself thereby. Do not altogether abstain from wine and flesh, for these things are not to be viewed with abhorrence, since [the Scripture] saith, "Ye shall eat the good things of the earth." And again, "Ye shall eat flesh even as herbs." And again, "Wine maketh glad the heart of man, and oil exhilarates, and bread strengthens him." But all are to be used with moderation, as being the gifts of God. "For who shall eat or who shall drink without Him? For if anything be beautiful, it is His; and if anything be good, it is His."

THE EPISTLE TO HERO, *Chapter 1 (Albany, OR: Sage Software, 1995), p. 223.*

AUGUSTINE
(Bishop of Hippo who lived 354 to 430)

By eating and drinking we repair the daily decays of our body, until Thou destroyest both belly and meat, when Thou hast slain my emptiness with a wonderful fullness, and clothed this incorruptible with an eternal incorruption. But now the necessity is sweet unto me, against which sweetness I fight, that I be not taken captive; and carry on a daily war by fastings; often bringing my body into subjection and my pains are removed by pleasure. . . . Oft it is uncertain, whether it be the necessary care of the body which is yet asking for sustenance, or whether a voluptuous deceivableness of greediness is proffering its services. In this uncertainty the unhappy soul rejoiceth, and therein prepares an excuse to shield itself, glad that it appeareth not what sufficeth for the moderation of health, that under the cloak of health, it may disguise the matter of gratification. These temptations I daily endeavor to resist, and I call on Thy right hand, and to Thee do I refer my perplexities; because I have as yet no settled counsel herein.

THE CONFESSIONS *(New York: Washington Square Press, 1962), p. 198-199.*

✧

If I be asked what is my own opinion in this matter, I answer, after carefully pondering the question, that in the Gospels and Epistles, and the entire collection of books for our instruction called the New Testament, I see that fasting is enjoined. But I do not discover any rule definitely laid down by the Lord or by the apostles as to days on which we ought or ought not to fast. And by this I am persuaded that exemption from fasting on the seventh day is more suitable, not indeed to obtain, but to foreshadow, that eternal rest in which the true Sabbath is realized, and which is obtained only by faith, and by that righteousness whereby the daughter of the King is all glorious within.

LETTER XXXVI, *Chapter 11, quoted from the Electronic Bible Society CD ROM, Vol. 1.*

CYRIL OF JERUSALEM
(Bishop of Jerusalem who lived from 315 to 386)

Be not then henceforth a viper, but as thou hast been formerly a viper's brood, put off, saith he, the slough of thy former sinful life. For every serpent creeps into a hole and casts its old slough, and having rubbed off the old skin, grows young again in body. In like manner enter thou also through the strait and narrow gate, rub off thy former self by fasting, and drive out that which is destroying thee.

THE CATECHETICAL LECTURES OF OUR HOLY FATHER, CYRIL, ARCHBISHOP OF JERUSALEM, *Lecture iii, "On Baptism," paragraph 7, quoted from the Electronic Bible Society CD ROM, Vol. 1.*

MARTIN LUTHER
(German reformer who lived 1483 to 1546)

[From a sermon on Matthew 4:1ff. in 1524] Of fasting I say this: it is right to fast frequently in order to subdue and control the body. For when the stomach is full, the body does not serve for preaching, for praying, for studying, or for doing anything else that is good. Under such circumstances God's Word cannot remain. But one should not fast with a view to meriting something by it as by a good work.

WHAT LUTHER SAYS, *Vol. 1, compiled by Ewald M. Plass (St. Louis: Concordia Publishing House, 1959), p. 506.*

❖

[On the soberness of mind that Peter exhorts in 1 Peter 1:13, Luther comments on the varied needs of different people.] He fixes no definite time, how long we are to fast, as the pope has done, but leaves it to the individual so to fast as always to remain sober and not burden the body with gluttony, that he may remain in possession of reason and reflections and determine how much he must do to keep his body under control. For it is utterly idle to impose one command about this on a whole group and congregation, since we are so unlike one another: one strong, another weak in body, so that one must mortify the body more, another less, if it is to remain sound and fit for good service. . . . It is good to fast. But only that can be called true fasting when we give the body no more food than it needs to retain its health. Let the body work and be wary, lest the old ass become too wanton and going on the ice to dance, break a bone. The body should be curbed and should follow the spirit; it should not act like those who, when they are about to fast, at one sitting fill themselves so full of fish and the best of wine that their bellies are bloated.

WHAT LUTHER SAYS, *Vol. 1, compiled by Ewald M. Plass (St. Louis: Concordia Publishing House, 1959), p. 507.*

❖

Scripture places before us two kinds of fasting that are good. The first kind one accepts willingly for the purpose of checking the flesh by the spirit. Concerning this Saint Paul says: ". . . in labors, in watchings, in fastings . . ." (2 Cor. 6:5). The second is the kind one must endure and yet accept willingly. Concerning this St. Paul says: "Even unto this present hour we both hunger and thirst" (1 Cor. 4:11). And Christ says of it: "When the bridegroom shall be taken from them . . . then they shall fast" (Matt. 9:15).

WHAT LUTHER SAYS, Vol. 1, compiled by Ewald M. Plass (St. Louis: Concordia Publishing House, 1959), p. 508.

JOHN CALVIN
(Reformer of Geneva who lived 1509 to 1564)

To sum them up: whenever a controversy over religion arises which ought to be settled by either a synod or an ecclesiastical court, whenever there is a question about choosing a minister, whenever, finally, any difficult matter of great importance is to be discussed, or again when there appear the judgments of the Lord's anger (as pestilence, war, and famine)—'tis a holy ordinance and one salutary for all ages, that pastors urge the people to public fasting and extraordinary prayers.

INSTITUTES OF THE CHRISTIAN RELIGION, Vol. 2 (Philadelphia: The Westminster Press, 1960), p. 1241 (IV, xii, 14).

✧

Holy and lawful fasting has three objectives. We use it either to weaken and subdue the flesh that it may not act wantonly, or that we may be better prepared for prayers and holy meditations, or that it may be a testimony of our self-abasement before God when we wish to confess our guilt before him.

INSTITUTES OF THE CHRISTIAN RELIGION, *Vol. 2 (Philadelphia: The Westminster Press, 1960), p. 1241 (IV, xii, 15).*

❖

[Paul's word on the sex-fast in 1 Corinthians 7:5 shows that fasting serves prayer and is not an end in itself. After referring to Anna in Luke 2:37 and Nehemiah in Nehemiah 1:4 he says:] For this reason, Paul says that believers act rightly if they abstain for a time from the marriage bed, that they may be left freer for prayer and fasting. There he joins fasting with prayer as an aid to it, and warns that it is of no importance of itself except as it is applied to this end [1 Corinthians 7:5].

INSTITUTES OF THE CHRISTIAN RELIGION, *Vol. 2 (Philadelphia: The Westminster Press, 1960), p. 1241 (IV, xii, 17).*

❖

Throughout its course, the life of the godly indeed ought to be tempered with frugality and sobriety, so that as far as possible it bears some resemblance to a fast. But, in addition, there is another sort of fasting, temporary in character, when we withdraw something from the normal regimen of living, either for one day or for a definite time, and pledge ourselves to a tighter more severe restraint in diet than ordinarily.

INSTITUTES OF THE CHRISTIAN RELIGION, *Vol. 2 (Philadelphia: The Westminster Press, 1960), p. 1241 (IV, xii, 18).*

MATTHEW HENRY
(English Presbyterian pastor and Bible expositor who lived 1662 to 1714)

If the solemnities of our fasting, though frequent, long and severe, do not serve to put an edge upon devout affections, to quicken prayer, to increase Godly sorrow, and to alter the temper of our minds, and the course of our lives, for the better, they do not at all answer the intention, and God will not accept them as performed to Him.

A COMMENTARY ON THE WHOLE BIBLE, *Vol. 4 (New York: Funk and Wagnalls, n. d.), p. 1478.*

WILLIAM LAW
(English spiritual writer who lived 1668 to 1761)

If religion requires us sometimes to fast and deny our natural appetites, it is to lessen that struggle and war that is in our nature; it is to render our bodies fitter instruments of purity, and more obedient to the good motions of divine grace; it is to dry up the springs of our passions that war against the soul, to cool the flame of our blood, and render the mind more capable of divine meditations. So that although these abstinences give some pain to the body, yet they so lessen the power of bodily appetites and passions, and so increase our taste of spiritual joys, that even these severities of religion, when practiced with discretion, add much to the comfortable enjoyment of our lives.

A SERIOUS CALL TO A DEVOUT AND HOLY LIFE *(Grand Rapids: Wm. B. Eerdmans Publishing Co., 1966, orig. 1728), p. 112.*

JONATHAN EDWARDS
(New England pastor-theologian who lived 1703 to 1758)

I suppose there is scarcely a minister in this land, but from Sabbath to Sabbath used to pray that God would pour out his Spirit, and work a reformation and revival of religion in the country, and turn us from our intemperance, profaneness, uncleanness, worldliness and other sins; and we have kept from year to year days of public fasting and prayer to God, to acknowledge our backslidings, and humble ourselves for our sins, and to seek of God forgiveness and reformation: and now when so great and extensive a reformation is so suddenly and wonderfully accomplished, in those very things that we have sought to God for, shall we not acknowledge it?

SOME THOUGHTS CONCERNING THE REVIVAL, *in* THE WORKS OF JONATHAN EDWARDS, *Vol. 4 (New Haven: Yale University Press, 1972), p. 331.*

❖

The state of the times extremely requires a fullness of the divine Spirit in ministers, and we ought to give ourselves no rest till we have obtained it. And in order to [do] this, I should think ministers, above all persons, ought to be much in secret prayer and fasting, and also much in praying and fasting one with another. It seems to me it would be becoming the circumstances of the present day, if ministers in a neighborhood would often meet together and spend days in fasting and fervent prayer among themselves, earnestly seeking for those extraordinary supplies of divine grace from heaven, that we need at this day.

SOME THOUGHTS CONCERNING THE REVIVAL, *in* THE WORKS OF JONATHAN EDWARDS, *Vol. 4 (New Haven: Yale University Press, 1972), p. 507.*

❖

One thing more I would mention concerning fasting and prayer, wherein I think there has been a neglect in ministers; and that is that although they recommend and much insist on the duty of secret prayer, in their preaching; so little is said about secret fasting. It is a duty recommended by our Savior to his followers, just in like manner as secret prayer is; as may be seen by comparing the 5th and 6th vss. of the 6th chap. of Matt. with vss. 16-18. Though I don't suppose that secret fasting is to be practiced in a stated manner and steady course as secret prayer, yet it seems to me 'tis a duty that all professing Christians should practice, and frequently practice. There are many occasions of both a spiritual and temporal nature that do properly require it; and there are many particular mercies that we desire for ourselves or friends that it would be proper, in this manner, to seek of God.

SOME THOUGHTS CONCERNING THE REVIVAL, *in* THE WORKS OF JONATHAN EDWARDS, *Vol. 4 (New Haven: Yale University Press, 1972), p. 521.*

JOHN WESLEY
(English evangelist of the Great Awakening who lived 1703 to 1791)

The man who never fasts is no more in the way to heaven than the man who never prays.

"Causes of Inefficacy of Christianity," SERMONS ON SEVERAL OCCASIONS, *ed. Thomas Jackson, Vol. 2 (New York: T. Mason and G. Lane, 1840), p. 440.*

✦

[Fasting] is an help to prayer; particularly when we set apart larger portions of time for private prayer. Then especially it is that God is often pleased to lift up the souls of his servants above all the things of earth, and sometimes to rap them up, as it were, into the third heaven. And it is chiefly, as it is an help to prayer, that it has so frequently been found a means, in the hand of God, of confirming and increasing, not one virtue, not chastity only, (as some have idly imagined, without any ground either from Scripture, reason, or experience,) but also seriousness of spirit, earnestness, sensibility and tenderness of conscience, deadness to the world, and consequently the love of God, and every holy and heavenly affection.

"Sermon XXVII, On Our Lord's Sermon on the Mount," THE WORKS OF JOHN WESLEY, *Vol. 5 (Albany, OR: Sage Software, 1995), p. 441.*

Not that there is any natural or necessary connection between fasting, and the blessings God conveys thereby. But he will have mercy as he will have mercy; he will convey whatsoever seemeth him good by whatsoever means he is pleased to appoint. And he hath, in all ages, appointed this to be a means of averting his wrath, and obtaining whatever blessings we, from time to time, stand in need of.

"Sermon XXVII, On Our Lord's Sermon on the Mount," THE WORKS OF JOHN WESLEY, *Vol. 5 (Albany, OR: Sage Software, 1995), p 441.*

✧

But, if we desire this reward, let us beware . . . of fancying we merit anything of God by our fasting. We cannot be too often warned of this; inasmuch as a desire to "establish our own righteousness," to procure salvation of debt and not of grace, is so deeply rooted in all our hearts. Fasting is only a way which God hath ordained, wherein we wait for his unmerited mercy; and wherein, without any desert of ours, he hath promised freely to give us his blessing.

"Sermon XXVII, On Our Lord's Sermon on the Mount," THE
WORKS OF JOHN WESLEY, *Vol. 5 (Albany, OR: Sage Software,
1995), p. 449.*

ANDREW FULLER
(English Baptist pastor and writer who lived 1754 to 1815)

Fasting is supposed to be the ordinary practice of the
godly. Christ does not make light of it, but merely cautions
them against its abuses. . . . It is an appendage to prayer,
and designed to aid its importunity. It is humbling, and in
a manner, chastising ourselves before God. The spirit of it
is expressed in the following passages—"So do God to me
and more also, if I taste bread, or aught else, till the sun be
down." "Surely I will not come into the tabernacle of my
house, nor go up into my bed; I will not give sleep to mine
eyes, nor slumber to mine eyelids, until I find out a place
for the Lord, an habitation for the mighty God of Jacob."
No mention is made of the time, or how often the duty
should be attended to. . . . It is only a *means*, however; if
rested in as an *end*, it will be an abomination in the sight
of God.

THE COMPLETE WORKS OF THE REV. ANDREW FULLER, *Vol. 1
(Harrisonburg, VA: Sprinkle Publication, 1988, orig. 1844),
p. 583.*

ABRAHAM LINCOLN
(President of the United States 1861-1865)

Whereas, the Senate of the United States, devoutly recog-
nizing the Supreme authority and Just Government of
Almighty God, in all the affairs of men and of nations, has,

by a resolution, requested the President to designate and set apart a day for National prayer and humiliation:

And whereas, it is the duty of nations, as well as of men, to own their dependence upon the overruling power of God, to confess their sins and transgressions, in humble sorrow, yet with assured hope that genuine repentance will lead to mercy and pardon; and to recognize the sublime truth, announced in the Holy Scriptures and proven by all history, that those nations only are blessed whose God is the Lord:

And, insomuch as we know that, by His divine law, nations, like individuals, are subjected to punishment and chastisements in this world, may we not justly fear that the awful calamity of civil war, which now desolates the land, may be but a punishment inflicted upon us for our presumptuous sins, to the needful end of our national reformation as a whole People? We have been the recipients of the choicest bounties of heaven. We have been preserved, these many years, in peace and prosperity. We have grown in numbers, wealth, and power as no other nation has ever grown. But we have forgotten God. We have forgotten the gracious hand which preserved us in peace, and multiplied and enriched and strengthened us; and we have vainly imagined, in the deceitfulness of our hearts, that all these blessings were produced by some superior wisdom and virtue of our own. Intoxicated with unbroken success, we have become too self-sufficient to feel the necessity of redeeming and preserving grace, too proud to pray to the God that made us! It behooves us, then, to humble ourselves before the offended Power, to confess our national sins, and to pray for clemency and forgiveness.

Now, therefore, in compliance with the request, and fully concurring in the views of the Senate, I do, by this my proclamation, designate and set apart Thursday, the 30th day of April, 1863, as a day of national humiliation, fasting, and prayer. And I do hereby request all the People to abstain on that day from their ordinary secular pursuits, and to unite, at their several places of public worship and their respective homes, in keeping the day holy to the Lord, and devoted to the humble discharge of the religious duties proper to that solemn occasion.

All this being done, in sincerity and truth, let us then rest humbly in the hope authorized by the divine teachings that the united cry of the nation will be heard on high, and answered with blessings, no less than the pardon of our national sins, and restoration of our now divided and suffering country, to its former happy condition of unity and peace.

In witness whereof, I have hereunto set my hand, and caused the seal of the United States to be affixed. Done at the city of Washington this thirtieth day of March, in the year of our Lord one thousand eight hundred and sixty-three, and of the Independence of the United States the eighty-seventh. Abraham Lincoln

Library of Congress, Appendix No. 19, Vol. 12 of THE UNITED STATES AT LARGE quoted in Derek Prince, SHAPING HISTORY THROUGH PRAYER AND FASTING (Old Tappan, NJ: Fleming H. Revell Company, 1973), pp. 5-8. For proclamations by George Washington, John Adams, and James Madison, see. pp. 138-147.

J. C. RYLE
(Evangelical bishop of Liverpool who lived 1816 to 1900)

Let us learn from our Lord's instruction about fasting, the great importance of cheerfulness in our religion. Those words, "anoint thy head, and wash thy face," are full of deep meaning. They should teach us to aim at letting men see that we find Christianity makes us happy. Never let us forget that there is not religion in looking melancholy and gloomy. Are we dissatisfied with Christ's wages, and Christ's service? Surely not! Then let us not look as if we were.

RYLE'S EXPOSITORY THOUGHTS ON THE GOSPELS, MATTHEW-MARK *(Grand Rapids: Zondervan Publishing House, n.d.), p.57.*

PHILLIPS BROOKS
(American pastor,
author of "O Little Town of Bethlehem," 1835-1893)

This, then, is the philosophy of fasting. It expresses repentance, and it uncovers the life to God. "Come down, my pride; stand back my passions; for I am wicked, and I wait for God to bless me."

"Fasting" (a sermon for Lent), in: THE CANDLE OF THE LORD AND OTHER SERMONS *(New York: E. P. Dutton and Company, 1881), p. 207.*

PASTOR HSI
(Chinese pastor in the nineteenth century)

[He made a medication in his ministry to opium-addicted Chinese.] Whenever it was necessary to make a fresh supply, he began with prayer and fasting. It was his habit to go without food the whole twenty-four hours of the day given to that work. Sometimes he was so exhausted towards the evening that he could hardly stand. Then he would go away for a few minutes alone to wait upon God. "Lord, it is Thy work. Give me Thy strength," was his plea. And he always came back fresh and reinvigorated, as if with food and rest.

Mrs. Howard M. Taylor, PASTOR HSI *(Singapore: Overseas Missionary Fellowship, 1989, orig. 1900), p. 131.*

PRAYING (JOHN) HYDE
(missionary to India at the turn of the twentieth century)

[At the Sialkot Convention in India for missionaries at the end of the nineteenth century John Hyde spent the whole time of the convention in the prayer room.] What about his meals, and his bed? The Convention lasted for ten days in those early days, and his "boy," a lad about sixteen that he had taken to his home and his heart, had brought Hyde's bedding and had carefully made his bed, but it was never used during the Convention. I saw him more than once when the prayer room was full, go aside into one of the corners and throw himself on the floor to sleep, but if the room began to get empty and prayer to flag, he somehow seemed to know it and was up immediately and took his place with the other intercessors. Did he go to his meals? I think it was only once or twice that I saw him with us at table. Sometimes his "boy," or Gulla, the sweeper, or one of his friends would take a plate of curry and rice or something else to him to the prayer room, and if convenient he would go to a corner and eat it. How his "boy" used to cry because he would not eat properly and would not go to bed to sleep.

E. G. *Carre,* PRAYING HYDE: A CHALLENGE TO PRAYER *(South Plainfield, NJ: Bridge Publishing, Inc., n.d.), p. 92.*

ANDREW MURRAY
(South African pastor and missionary statesman, 1828-1916)

Prayer needs fasting for its full growth. Prayer is the one hand with which we grasp the invisible. Fasting is the other hand, the one with which we let go of the visible. In nothing is man more closely connected with the world of sense than in this need for, and enjoyment of, food. It was the fruit with which man was tempted and fell in Paradise. It was with bread that

Jesus was tempted in the wilderness. But He triumphed in fasting. . . . The body has been redeemed to be a temple of the Holy Spirit. In body as well as spirit, Scripture says, we are to glorify God in eating and drinking. There are many Christians to whom this eating for the glory of God has not yet become a spiritual reality. The first thought suggested by Jesus' words in regard to fasting and prayer is that only in a life of moderation and self-denial will there be sufficient heart and strength to pray much. . . . Fasting helps to express, to deepen, and to confirm the resolution that we are ready to sacrifice anything, even ourselves, to attain the Kingdom of God. And Jesus, Who Himself fasted and sacrificed, knows to value, accept, and reward with spiritual power the soul that is thus ready to give up everything for Him and His Kingdom.

WITH CHRIST IN THE SCHOOL OF PRAYER *(Springdale, PA: Whitaker House, 1981), pp. 100-101.*

DIETRICH BONHOEFFER
(twentieth-century German theologian and martyr)

Jesus takes it for granted that his disciples will observe the pious custom of fasting. Strict exercise of self-control is an essential feature of the Christian's life. Such customs have only one purpose—to make the disciples more ready and cheerful to accomplish those things which God would have done.

THE COST OF DISCIPLESHIP *(New York: Collier Books / Macmillan Publishing Co., 1949), p. 188.*

When the flesh is satisfied it is hard to pray with cheerfulness or to devote oneself to a life of service which calls for much self-renunciation.

THE COST OF DISCIPLESHIP *(New York: Collier Books / Macmillan Publishing Co., 1949), p. 189.*

✧

We have to practice strictest daily discipline; only so can the flesh learn the painful lesson that it has no rights of its own.

THE COST OF DISCIPLESHIP *(New York: Collier Books / Macmillan Publishing Co., 1949), p. 189.*

C. S. LEWIS
(English Literature professor and Christian writer, 1898-1963)

It is impossible to accept Christianity for the sake of finding comfort: but the Christian tries to lay himself open to the will of God, to do what God wants him to do. You don't know in advance whether God is going to set you to do something difficult or painful, or something that you will quite like; and some people of heroic mould are disappointed when the job doled out to them turns out to be something quite nice. But you must be prepared for the unpleasant things and the discomforts. I don't mean fasting, and things like that. They are a different matter. When you are training soldiers in maneuvers, you practice in blank ammunition because you would like them to have practices before meeting the real enemy. So we must practice in abstaining from pleasures which are not in themselves wicked. If you don't abstain from pleasure, you won't be good when the time comes along. It is purely a matter of practice.

GOD IN THE DOCK *(Grand Rapids: Wm. B. Eerdmans Publishing Co., 1970), pp. 53-54.*

MARTYN LLOYD-JONES
(twentieth-century preacher in London)

Fasting, if we conceive of it truly, must not . . . be confined to the question of food and drink; fasting should really be made to include abstinence from anything which is legitimate in and of itself for the sake of some special spiritual purpose. There are many bodily functions which are right and normal and perfectly legitimate, but which for special peculiar reasons in certain circumstances should be controlled. That is fasting.

STUDIES IN THE SERMON ON THE MOUNT, *Vol. 2 (Grand Rapids: Wm. B. Eerdmans Publishing Co., 1960), p. 38.*

DAVID R. SMITH
(twentieth-century author)

A selfish person is unable to enjoy the gospel; a Christian is someone who has begun to deny himself, and is in the continuous process of denying himself. Jesus said "If any man will come after Me, let him deny himself, and take up his cross, and follow Me." Self-denial is not limited to one particular kind of giving; it embraces all personal disciplines. Fasting is only one discipline; nevertheless, it is self-denial. This does not mean that to fast is to embrace legalism; it is gospel liberty which encourages us to deny ourselves.

FASTING: A NEGLECTED DISCIPLINE *(Fort Washington, PA: Christian Literature Crusade, 1954), p. 17.*

✧

Nobody can maintain a desired state of mind whilst his bodily condition is not in accordance with it. If a man is anxious to devote himself to spiritual things, for a time, he is obliged to ensure that his body is in similar environment, or else he may not succeed. He cannot be reverent in the midst of his own physical irreverence. Fasting ensures the correct environment for sorrowful and serious considerations. Asterius wrote, in the 4th Century, that one role of fasting is to ensure that the stomach does not make the body boil like a kettle, to the hindering of the soul.

FASTING: A NEGLECTED DISCIPLINE *(Fort Washington, PA: Christian Literature Crusade, 1954), pp. 38-39.*

✧

Fasting does not *create* faith, for faith grows in us as we hear, and read, and dwell upon, God's Word; it is a work of the Holy Spirit to bring faith to God's people. However, fasting has the capacity to *encourage* faith in the one who is involved in this discipline. It seems as though the neglect of self feeds the faith which God has implanted in the hearts of born-again believers. This doesn't mean that those who eat the least have the most faith; such a view is not only untrue, it is extremist. It is simply that regular self-denial has its benefits, and one of these is seen in a personal increase in faith.

FASTING: A NEGLECTED DISCIPLINE *(Fort Washington, PA: Christian Literature Crusade, 1954), pp. 47-48.*

KEITH MAIN

(twentieth-century writer)

To Judaism, a fast was an *outward* sign of an inward condition. To Jesus, a fast was an *inward* sign of an inward condition. The former, if misused, "a peculiarly ugly form of religious dramatic art," the latter a part of "closet" devotions.

PRAYER AND FASTING: A STUDY IN THE DEVOTIONAL LIFE OF THE
EARLY CHURCH *(New York: Carlton Press, Inc., 1971), p. 37.*

Thus far we have suggested that the joy and thanksgiving that marks the prayer life of the New Testament is a sign of the inbreaking of the Kingdom of God. Fasting is no longer consistent with the joyous and thankful attitude that marks the fellowship. Yet this is only partially so. . . . It is true that the crisis and the tragedy are there as a stark reality. The Kingdom is not *fully* realized. Granted that the Bridegroom is present and now is not an appropriate time to mourn. Yet this is not entirely so, for we are still in the flesh and weak in faith. . . . Within this "bitter struggle" the believer, in this devotional life, might conceivably find occasion to fast. It would be only one among many of the ingredients that go to make up the life of the man in Christ. One might read through 2 Corinthians 6:3-10 and 11:23-29 for a glimpse into the wide range of such suffering in the "bitter struggle" for the cause of Christ. Against such a background the "hungers" mentioned in 6:5 and 11:27 gain their true perspective.

PRAYER AND FASTING: A STUDY IN THE DEVOTIONAL LIFE OF THE
EARLY CHURCH *(New York: Carlton Press, Inc., 1971), pp. 83-84.*

RICHARD J. FOSTER
(twentieth-century devotional writer)

It is well to know the process your body goes through in the course of a longer fast. The first three days are usually the most difficult in terms of physical discomfort and hunger pains. The body is beginning to rid itself of the toxic poisons that have built up over years of poor eating habits, and it is not a comfortable process. This is the reason for the coating of the tongue and bad breath. Do not be disturbed by these symptoms; rather be grateful for the increased health and wellbeing that will result. You may experience headaches during this time, especially if you are an avid coffee or tea drinker. Those are mild withdrawal symptoms which will pass, though they may be very unpleasant for a time.

By the fourth day the hunger pains are beginning to subside though you will have feelings of weakness and occasional dizziness. The dizziness is only temporary and caused by sudden changes in position. Move more slowly and you will have no difficulty. The weakness can come to the point where the simplest task takes great effort. Rest is the best remedy. Many find this the most difficult period of the fast.

By the sixth or seventh day you will begin to feel stronger and more alert. Hunger pains will continue to diminish until by the ninth or tenth day they are only a minor irritation. The body will have eliminated the bulk of toxic poisons and you will feel good. Your sense of concentration will be sharpened and you will feel as if you could continue fasting indefinitely. Physically this is the most enjoyable part of the fast.

Anywhere from twenty-one to forty days or longer, depending upon the individual, hunger pains will return. This is the first stage of starvation and signals that the body has used up all its excess reserves and is beginning to draw on the living tissue. The fast should be broken at this time.

THE CELEBRATION OF DISCIPLINE *(New York: Harper and Row, Publishers, 1978), pp. 51-52.*

DALLAS WILLARD
(twentieth-century writer on the spiritual disciplines)

Fasting is a hard discipline to practice without its consuming all our attention. Yet when we use it as a part of prayer or service, we cannot allow it to do so. When a person chooses fasting as a spiritual discipline, he or she must, then, practice it well enough and often enough to become experienced in it, because only the person who is well habituated to systematic fasting as a discipline can use it effectively as a part of direct service to God, as in special times of prayer or other service.

THE SPIRIT OF THE DISCIPLINES: UNDERSTANDING HOW GOD CHANGES LIVES *(San Francisco: Harper and Row, 1988), p. 168.*

JOSEPH F. WIMMER
(twentieth-century writer)

[On Mark 2:18-22 and the bridegroom's presence and absence:] Their non-fasting was intended to make a point, namely that the eschatological age had come in Jesus. . . . The future return to fasting after his being "taken away" was therefore also related to Jesus, as a sad memorial of what happened on that fateful Friday, mixed with inner confidence and humble trust in his second coming and the final consummation of the parousia. This Christian fast was something new, distinct from that of Judaism, not only as regards the day of fasting, but more importantly, in terms of its inner motivation. Even as a sign of humble worship of the Father it was henceforth related to Jesus, through whom our salvation has come, and in whose presence we will one day rejoice without reservation, in the plenitude of his Kingdom.

FASTING IN THE NEW TESTAMENT: A BIBLICAL THEOLOGY *(New York: Paulist Press, 1982), p. 101.*

The weakness of hunger which leads to death brings forth the goodness and power of God who wills life. Here there is no extortion, no magic attempt to force God's will. We merely look with confidence upon our heavenly Father and through our fasting say gently in our hearts: "Father, without you I will die; come to my assistance, make haste to help me."

FASTING IN THE NEW TESTAMENT: A BIBLICAL THEOLOGY *(New York: Paulist Press, 1982), p. 119.*

ADALBERT DE VOGÜÉ
(twentieth-century Monk of the Abbey of La Pierre-qui-Vire, France)

The beneficial results of the fast are felt first in the sexual sphere. I have easily verified the connection established by the Ancients between the first two "principal vices," gluttony and lust, and consequently between the corresponding disciplines: fasting and chastity. Fasting is the most effective help for a religious who has vowed chastity. Fantasies no longer appear even during the happy hours of physiological freedom of which I have spoken, and the rest of the time they are easily controlled and eliminated.

TO LOVE FASTING: THE MONASTIC EXPERIENCE *(Petersham, MA: Saint Bede's Publications, 1989), p. 10.*

It will surprise no one if I confess that I am subject to anxiety and irritation, sadness and nervousness, to say nothing of vanity, touchiness or envy. . . . The habit of fasting effects a profound appeasement of all these instinctive movements. I think the cause is that a certain mastery of the primordial appetite, eating, permits a greater mastery of the other manifestations of the libido and aggressiveness. It is as if the man who fasts were more himself, in possession of his true identity, and less dependent on exterior objects and the impulses they arouse in him. . . . Among the lesser advantages, let us note only the time saved in sitting down to table once instead of three times.

TO LOVE FASTING: THE MONASTIC EXPERIENCE *(Petersham, MA: Saint Bede's Publications, 1989), p. 10.*

✧

To love fasting is not only possible. In the light of the facts, I will go so far as to say that the contrary appears impossible to me, to whatever degree one has truly experienced fasting. Experience fasting, and you will love it.

TO LOVE FASTING: THE MONASTIC EXPERIENCE *(Petersham, MA: Saint Bede's Publications, 1989), p. 104.*

ARTHUR WALLIS
(twentieth-century devotional writer)

Almost all are agreed that a visitation of the spirit upon the Church is desperately needed. Are we to believe the promise to Joel has nothing to say to this situation? . . . Did the events at Pentecost exhaust the Joel prophecy? Obviously not, or there would have been no further outpourings. . . . If however we believe this wonderful promise is for us—is in fact God's answer to the present need—it is vital that we fulfill the conditions as well as plead the promise. Three times Joel sounds a clarion call, in view of the imminence of the Day of the Lord, to return to God *with fasting* (Joel 1:14; 2:12, 15). Then he seems to see in vision God's response: "Then the Lord became jealous for his land, and had pity on this people" (v. 18).

GOD'S CHOSEN FAST: A SPIRITUAL AND PRACTICAL GUIDE TO FASTING *(Fort Washington, PA: Christian Literature Crusade, 1968), pp. 131-132.*

WESLEY DUEWEL
(twentieth-century writer on prayer)

You and I have no more right to omit fasting because we feel no special emotional prompting than we have a right to omit prayer, Bible reading, or assembling with God's children for lack of some special emotional prompting. Fasting is just as biblical and normal a part of a spiritual walk of obedience with God as are these others.

MIGHTY PREVAILING PRAYER *(Grand Rapids: Zondervan/Francis Asbury Press, 1990), p. 184.*

✧

How do you take up your cross? To take up a cross is not to have someone place the cross upon you. Sickness, persecution, and the antagonism of other people are not your real cross. To take up a cross is a deliberate choice. We must purposely humble ourself [sic], stoop down, and pick up the cross for Jesus. Fasting is one of the most biblical ways to do so.

MIGHTY PREVAILING PRAYER *(Grand Rapids: Zondervan/Francis Asbury Press, 1990), p. 184.*

✧

Fasting can deepen hunger for God to work. Spiritual hunger and fasting have a reciprocal power. Each deepens and strengthens the other. Each makes the other more effective. When your spiritual hunger becomes very deep, you may even lose the desire for food. All of the most intense forms of prevailing prayer . . . can be deepened, clarified, and greatly empowered by fasting.

Fasting is natural when you are burdened sufficiently, wrestling with mighty prevailings, and warring in hand-to-hand conflict with Satan and his powers of darkness. Fasting becomes sweet and blessed as your hunger reaches out to God. Your hunger gains tremendous power as you fast and pray—particularly if you set apart time from all else to give yourself to fasting and prayer. It can become a spiritual joy to fast.

MIGHTY PREVAILING PRAYER *(Grand Rapids: Zondervan/Francis Asbury Press, 1990), p. 188.*

✦

Fasting feeds your faith. . . . Your confidence begins to deepen. Your hope begins to rise, for you know you are doing what pleases the Lord. Your willingness to deny self and voluntarily to take up this added cross kindles an inner joy. Your faith begins to lay hold of God's promise more simply and more firmly.

MIGHTY PREVAILING PRAYER *(Grand Rapids: Zondervan/Francis Asbury Press, 1990), p. 189.*

J. OSWALD SANDERS
(twentieth-century missionary statesman)

Fasting is not a legalistic requirement but a spontaneous reaction under special circumstances. . . . There are . . . godly and prayerful people who have found fasting a hindrance rather than a help. Some are so constituted physically that the lack of a minimum amount of food renders them unable to concentrate in prayer. . . . There is no need for such to be in bondage. Let them do what most helps them to pray.

PRAYER POWER UNLIMITED *(Chicago: Moody Press, 1977), p. 67.*

EDITH SCHAEFFER
(twentieth-century writer)

Is fasting ever a bribe to get God to pay more attention to the petitions? No, a thousand times no. It is simply a way to make clear that we sufficiently reverence the amazing opportunity to ask help from the everlasting God, the Creator of the universe, to choose to put everything else aside and concentrate on worshiping, asking for forgiveness, and making our requests known—considering His help more important than anything we could do ourselves in our own strength and with our own ideas.

THE LIFE OF PRAYER *(Wheaton: Crossway Books, 1992), pp. 75-76.*

JERRY FALWELL
(twentieth-century Baptist pastor)

An old saint once said that fasting prevents luxuries from becoming necessities. Fasting is a protection of the spirit against the encroachments of the body. When a person fasts, he has his body well in hand, and is able to do the work of the Master.

FASTING: WHAT THE BIBLE TEACHES *(Wheaton, IL: Tyndale House Publishers, Inc., 1981), p. 11.*

BILL BRIGHT
*(twentieth-century evangelist
and founder of Campus Crusade for Christ)*

It will take nothing short of the supernatural to stem the tides of judgment devastating our land. I believe that nothing else can compare with the supernatural power released when we fast and pray. We know for certain from Hebrews 11:6 and from personal experience that God rewards those who diligently seek Him.

THE COMING REVIVAL: AMERICA'S CALL TO FAST, PRAY AND "SEEK GOD'S FACE" *(Orlando, FL: New Life Publications, 1995), pp. 108.*

CORNELIUS PLANTINGA, JR.
(twentieth-century theologian)

Self-indulgence is the enemy of gratitude, and self-discipline usually its friend and generator. That is why gluttony is a deadly sin. The early desert fathers believed that a person's appetites are linked: full stomachs and jaded palates take the edge from our hunger and thirst for righteousness. They spoil the appetite for God.

Quoted from THE REFORMED JOURNAL, *Nov. 1988, in Donald S. Whitney,* SPIRITUAL DISCIPLINES FOR THE CHRISTIAN LIFE *(Colorado Springs: NavPress, 1991), p. 151.*

BIBLIOGRAPHY

The books listed here are a selected resource for further study. The list is neither exhaustive, nor uniformly commendable. "Test all things and hold fast to what is good" (1 Thessalonians 5:21).

Anderson, Andy, *Fasting Changed My Life*. Nashville, TN: Broadman Press, 1977.

Beall, James Lee, *The Adventure of Fasting*. Old Tappan, NJ: Fleming H. Revell Company, 1974.

Benson, Bob, and Michael W. Benson, "Fasting," *Disciplines for the Inner Life*. Waco, TX: Word Books, 1985.

Bragg, Paul C., *The Miracle of Fasting: Proven Throughout History*. Desert Hot Springs, CA: Health Science, 1976.

Bright, Bill, *The Coming Revival: America's Call to Fast, Pray, and "Seek God's Face."* Orlando, FL: New Life Publications, 1995.

Brooks, Phillips, "Fasting" (A sermon for Lent) in: *The Candle of the Lord and Other Sermons*. New York: E. P. Dutton and Company, 1881.

Carruth, Thomas A., *Forty Days of Fasting and Prayer*. Wilmore, KY: Asbury Seminary, 1974.

Charles, Jerry, *God's Guide to Fasting: A Complete and Exhaustive Biblical Encyclopedia*. Madison, NC: Power Press, 1977.

Chatham, R. D., *Fasting: A Biblical-Historical Study*. South Plainfield, NJ: Bridge Publishing, Inc., 1987.

Cott, Allan, *Fasting as a Way of Life*. New York: Bantam Books, 1977

DeWelt, Don, and John E. Baird, *What the Bible Says About Fasting*. Joplin, MO: College Press Publishing Co., 1984.

Duewel, Wesley L. "You Can Deepen Your Prayer by Fasting," in: *Touch the World Through Prayer*. Grand Rapids: Zondervan/Francis Asbury Press, 1986.

Duewel, Wesley L. "Jesus Said They Would Fast" and "Fasting Strengthens Prayer," in: *Mighty Prevailing Prayer*. Grand Rapids: Zondervan/ Francis Asbury Press, 1990.

Falwell, Jerry, *Fasting: What the Bible Teaches*. Wheaton, IL: Tyndale House Publishers, Inc., 1981.

Foster, Richard, "Fasting," in: *The Celebration of Discipline*. New York: Harper and Row, Publishers, 1978, pp. 41-53.

Lindsay, Gordon, *Prayer and Fasting*. Dallas: Christ for the Nations, 1972.

Lloyd-Jones, Martyn, "Fasting," in: *Studies in the Sermon on the Mount*, Vol. 2, Grand Rapids: Wm. B. Eerdmans Publishing Co., 1960, pp. 33-44.

Main, Keith, *Prayer and Fasting: A Study in the Devotional Life of the Early Church*. New York: Carlton Press, Inc., 1971.

Maloney, George A., *A Return to Fasting*. Pecos, NM: Dove Publications, 1974.

Miller, James, *Systematic Fasting*. Indianapolis: James Miller, n.d.

Massey, James Earl, *Spiritual Disciplines: Growth through the Practice of Prayer, Fasting, Dialogue and Worship*. Grand Rapids: Zondervan Publishing House, 1985.

Prince, Derek, *Shaping History Through Prayer and Fasting*. Old Tappan, NJ: Fleming H. Revell Company, 1973.

Rogers, Eric N., *Fasting: The Phenomenon of Self-denial*. Nashville, TN: Thomas Nelson, Publishers, 1976.

Ryan, Thomas, *Fasting Rediscovered*. New York: Paulist Press, 1981.

Smith, David R., *Fasting A Neglected Discipline*. Fort Washington, PA: Christian Literature Crusade, 1954.

Smith, Fredrick W., *Journal of a Fast*. New York: Schocken Books, 1976.

Wallis, Arthur, *God's Chosen Fast*. Fort Washington, PA: Christian Literature Crusade, 1968.

Wesley, John, "Sermon XXVII, On Our Lord's Sermon on the Mount," in: *The Works of John Wesley*, Vol. 5. Albany, OR: Sage Software, 1995.

Whitney, Donald, "Fasting," in: *Spiritual Disciplines for the Christian Life*. Colorado Springs, CO: NavPress, 1991, pp. 151-172.

Willard, Dallas, *The Spirit of the Disciplines: Understanding How God Changes Lives*. San Francisco: Harper and Row, 1988.

Wimmer, Joseph, *Fasting in the New Testament: A Biblical Theology*. New York: Paulist Press, 1982.

NOTES

INTRODUCTION
(pages 12-23)

1. Quoted in Thomas Ryan, *Fasting Rediscovered* (New York: Paulist Press, 1981), p. 44.

2. Martyn Lloyd-Jones, *Studies in the Sermon on the Mount*, Vol. 2 (Grand Rapids: Wm. B. Eerdmans Publishing Co., 1960), p. 38.

3. The word that I translate "bid farewell" is used five other times in the New Testament, and the meaning of each of these is to "take leave of" or "to bid farewell to" (Mark 6:46; Luke 9:61; Acts 18:18, 21; 2 Corinthians 2:13). The point is that we can only use our possessions aright when we have been freed from them as necessary to our contentment in God.

4. C. S. Lewis, *The Problem of Pain* (New York: The Macmillan Co., 1962), pp. 101-102.

5. St. Augustine, *The City of God*, Book XVI, Section 32 (New York: Random House Inc., 1950), p. 554.

6. Richard Foster, *The Celebration of Discipline* (New York: Harper and Row Publishers, 1978), p. 48.

7. Ibid., p. 48.

8. C. S. Lewis, *Letters of C. S. Lewis*, ed. W. H. Lewis (New York: Harcourt Brace and World, Inc., 1966), p. 289.

9. Similarly Phillips Brooks said, "The more we watch the lives of men, the more we see that one of the reasons why men are not occupied with great thoughts and interest is the way in which their lives are overfilled with little things." Phillips Brooks, "Fasting" (a sermon for Lent) in: *The Candle of the Lord and Other Sermons* (New York: E. P. Dutton and Company, 1881), p. 207.

CHAPTER ONE
(pages 24-49)

1. Didache, VIII, quoted from The Apostolic Fathers (Loeb Classical Library), translated by Kirsopp Lake (London: William Heinemann, Ltd., 1970), p. 321.

2. Richard Foster is almost willing to say this much, but not quite. Referring to Matthew 9:14-17, he says, "That is perhaps the most important statement in the New Testament on whether Christians should fast today." Richard Foster, *The Celebration of Discipline* (New York: Harper and Row, Publishers, 1978), p. 46. The parallels to this passage are Mark 2:18-22 and Luke 5:33-39.

3. "Fasting," by Richard T. Foster, in *New Dictionary of Christian Ethics and Pastoral Theology*, eds. David J. Atkinson, David F. Field, Arthur Holmes, Oliver O'Donovan (Downers Grove, IL: InterVarsity Press, 1995), p. 376.

4. "Probably no single cause can be alleged as the origin of the practice of fasting." "Fasting," by A. J. Maclean, in *Encyclopedia of Religion and Ethics*, ed. James Hastings (New York: Charles Scribner's Sons, 1912), p. 759.

5. The Hebrew idiom in Leviticus, "humble (or afflict) the soul," was taken by the Jews as a call for fasting, and so this day became the central fast in Jewish history. Psalm 35:13 shows this connection between "afflicting the soul" and fasting: "I humbled (or afflicted) my soul with fasting." This is probably "the fast" that Luke referred to in Acts 27:9.

6. Eric N. Rogers has a chapter on how each of these religions fasts, *Fasting, The Phenomenon of Self-denial* (Nashville: Thomas Nelson Inc. Publishers, 1976), Part II, Chapters 4, 6, 7.

7. *Encyclopedia of Religion and Ethics*, pp. 760-761.

8. Quoted in *The Phenomenon of Self-denial*, pp. 77-78.

9. Ibid., pp. 79-80.

10. The tragedy of this condition can be seen in the testimony of one young woman: "All I want is to become thinner and thinner, but I don't want to pay attention to it continuously, and I do not want to miss anything. It is this eternal tension between wanting to be thin and not to give up eating that is so exhausting. In all other points I am reasonable, but I know on this point I am crazy." Quoted in ibid., p. 135.

11. George Ladd, *The Presence of the Future* (Grand Rapids: Wm. B. Eerdmans Publishing Co., 1974), p. 225 (italics in the original).

12. Keith Main, *Prayer and Fasting: A Study in the Devotional Life of the Early Church* (New York: Carlton Press, Inc., 1971), p. 84 (italics added).

13. The references to fasting outside the Gospels are Acts 13:2-3; 14:23; 2 Corinthians 6:5; 11:27. The references in the King James Version of 1 Corinthians 7:5 and Acts 10:30 are probably not in the oldest and best Greek manuscripts.

14. *Prayer and Fasting: A Study in the Devotional Life of the Early Church*, pp. 54, 60-61.

15. C. S. Lewis, *The Problem of Pain* (New York: The Macmillan Co., 1962), p. 112.

16. Robert H. Gundry, *Matthew: A Commentary on His Literary and Theological Art* (Grand Rapids: Wm. B. Eerdmans Publishing Co., 1982), p. 169.

17. Arthur Wallis, *God's Chosen Fast* (Fort Washington, PA: Christian Literature Crusade, 1968), pp. 28-32.

18. See note 11.

19. See note 11.

20. I have tried to spell out this uniquely Christian dependence of the future grace of God on the past grace of God in *The Purifying Power of Living by Faith in Future Grace* (Sisters, OR: Multnomah Press, 1995), chapters 7-9.

21. This understanding of faith is developed and defended biblically in *Future Grace*, Chapters 14-16.

22. *Prayer and Fasting: A Study in the Devotional Life of the Early Church*, p. 83.

23. Ibid., p. 84.

24. The rare Greek word behind this phrase (*ethelothrēskia*) seems to connote the origin and maintenance of this "worship" or "religion" in the human will, rather than in the grace of God. It originates when one is not "holding fast to the head," namely, Christ, as the source of all things.

25. The word implies mainly sexual "continence." But its use in 1 Corinthians 9:25 shows that it has a broader meaning of discipline in all areas of life. "Everyone who competes in the games exercises self-control in all things."

26. *Prayer and Fasting: A Study in the Devotional Life of the Early Church*, p. 60.

27. The NASB translates this "often without food," as though it referred to involuntary hunger. But the fact that just before this word Paul mentions "in hunger and thirst" would suggest that something other than ordinary hunger is in view. Moreover the word used here (*nēsteiais*) is always used in the New Testament for religious fasting, and this is its regular meaning in the Greek Old Testament as well (about thirty times).

CHAPTER TWO

(pages 50-65)

1. Joseph F. Wimmer, *Fasting in the New Testament: A Biblical Theology* (New York: Paulist Press, 1982), p. 119.

2. Quoted in Richard Foster, *The Celebration of Discipline* (New York: Harper and Row, Publishers, 1978), p. 48.

3. Ibid., p. 48.

4. Joseph F. Wimmer, *Fasting in the New Testament: A Biblical Theology,* (New York: Paulist Press, 1982), p. 119.

5. Dietrich Bonhoeffer, *The Cost of Discipleship* (New York: Collier Books Macmillan Publishing Co., 1949), pp. 189-190.

CHAPTER THREE
(pages 66-81)

1. Quoted from St. Augustine, *The Confessions of St. Augustine,* in *Documents of the Christian Church,* ed. Henry Bettenson (London: Oxford University Press, 1967), p. 54.

2. J. C. Ryle, *Ryle's Expository Thoughts on the Gospels, Matthew–Mark* (Grand Rapids: Zondervan Publishing House, n.d.), p. 57.

3. Dietrich Bonhoeffer, *The Cost of Discipleship* (New York: Collier Books / Macmillan Publishing Co., 1949), p. 188.

4. Keith Main, *Prayer and Fasting: A Study in the Devotional Life of the Early Church* (New York: Carlton Press, Inc., 1971), p. 37.

5. John Piper, *Desiring God: Meditations of a Christian Hedonist* (Sisters, OR: Multnomah Press, 1996, revised edition), *The Pleasures of God: Meditations on God's Delight in Being God* (Sisters, OR: Multnomah Press, 1991), *The Purifying Power of Living by Faith in Future Grace* (Sisters, OR: Multnomah Press, 1995).

6. C.S. Lewis, *The Problem of Pain* (New York: The Macmillan Co., 1962), p. 145.

CHAPTER FOUR
(pages 82-97)

1. George Ladd, "A Motive for Mission," in *Pray for Tibet,* Vol. 2, No. 2, Summer 1991, pp. 4-6. The quote is taken from Ladd's book, *The Gospel of the Kingdom: Popular Exposition on the Kingdom of God* (Grand Rapids: Wm. B. Eerdmans Publishing, Co. 1959).

2. John Wesley, "Sermon XXVII, On Our Lord's Sermon on the Mount," in: *The Works of John Wesley,* Vol. 5 (Albany, OR: Sage Software, 1995), pp. 440-441.

3. See John Piper, *Let the Nations Be Glad: The Supremacy of God in*

Missions (Grand Rapids: Baker Book House, 1993), Chapter Five, "The Supremacy of God among 'All Nations.'"

4. Anthony Hoekema, *The Bible and the Future* (Grand Rapids: Wm. B. Eerdmans Publishing Co., 1979), p. 139.

5. George Ladd, "A Motive for Mission," pp. 4-6.

CHAPTER FIVE
(pages 98-123)

1. Jonathan Edwards, *Some Thoughts Concerning the Revival*, in *The Works of Jonathan Edwards*, Vol. 4 (New Haven: Yale University Press, 1972), p. 507.

2. Charles Finney, *Power from on High* (Albany, OR: Sage Software, 1995), pp. 9-10 (italics added).

3. On Asahel Nettleton's ministry and the comparison between him and Finney, see J. F. Thornbury, *God Sent Revival: The Story of Asahel Nettleton and the Second Great Awakening* (Grand Rapids: Evangelical Press, 1977), and Bennet Tyler and Andrew Bonar, *The Life and Labors of Asahel Nettleton* (Edinburgh: The Banner of Truth Trust, 1975, orig. 1854).

4. See the perceptive assessment of Finney's ministry and theology in John MacArthur, Jr., *Ashamed of the Gospel* (Wheaton, IL: Crossway Books, 1993), pp. 227-235. "I was often instrumental in bringing Christians under great conviction, and into a state of temporary repentance and faith. . . . [But] falling short of urging them up to a point, where they would become so acquainted with Christ as to abide in him, they would of course soon relapse into their former state" (p. 235). With regard to his view of God's sovereignty in relation to the will of man, see his criticisms of Jonathan Edwards in Charles Finney, *Finney's Systematic Theology* (Minneapolis: Bethany Fellowship, Inc., 1976, orig. 1846), pp. 256-299. With regard to the long-term effects of Finney's views, I would tend to agree with the view that, while leading many to Christ, "Finney's real legacy is the disastrous impact he had on American evangelical theology and evangelistic methodology. The church in our generation is still seething with the leaven Finney introduced, and modern evangelical pragmatism is proof of that" (MacArthur, p. 235).

5. Wesley Duewel, *Mighty Prevailing Prayer* Grand Rapids: Zondervan/Francis Asbury Press, 1990), p. 192.

6. John Wesley, *The Journal of Rev. John Wesley* (London: The Epworth Press, 1938), p. 147.

7. David Bryant, *The Hope at Hand: National and World Revival for the Twenty-First Century* (Grand Rapids: Baker Book House, 1995), p. 127. See pp. 127-142 and 231-244.

8. Jonathan Edwards, *Some Thoughts Concerning the Revival*, in *The Works of Jonathan Edwards*, Vol. 4 (New Haven: Yale University Press, 1972), p. 507.

9. Ibid., p. 521.

10. Ibid., p. 516. An interesting sidelight is that Jonathan Edwards observed that in his day the people had gathered themselves into what we today would call "small groups" and so he promoted prayer and fasting among these groups as well: "The inhabitants of many of our towns are now divided into particular praying societies; most of the people, young and old, have voluntarily associated themselves in distinct companies, for mutual assistance in social worship, in private houses: what I intend therefore is that days of prayer should be spent partly in these distinct praying companies. Such a method of keeping a fast as this, has several times been proved; viz. in the forenoon, after the duties of the family and closet, as societies; companies of men by themselves, and companies of women by themselves; young men by themselves, and young women by themselves; and companies of children in all parts of the town by themselves. As many as were capable of social religious exercises; the boys by themselves, and girls by themselves . . . and about the middle of the day, at an appointed hour, all have met together in the house of God, to offer up public prayers, and to hear a sermon suitable to the occasion: and then, they have retired from the house of God again in their private societies, and spent the remaining part of the day in praying together there, excepting so much as was requisite for the duties of the family and closet in their own houses." Ibid., p. 519.

11. Ibid., p. 353.

12. Jonathan Edwards, *The Distinguishing Marks of a Work of the Spirit of God*, in *The Works of Jonathan Edwards*, Vol. 4 (New Haven: Yale University Press, 1972), p. 282.

13. *Some Thoughts Concerning the Revival*, p. 345.

14. *Jonathan Edwards, The Life of David Brainerd*, ed. Norman Pettit, *The Works of Jonathan Edwards*, Vol. 7 (New Haven: Yale University Press, 1985), p. 162 (italics added).

15. Ibid., p. 531.

16. Cotton Mather, *The Great Works of Christ in America*, Vol. 2 (Edinburgh: The Banner of Truth Trust, 1979, orig. 1702), p.148 (italics added).

17. Richard Lovelace, "Cotton Mather," in *Eerdman's Handbook to Christianity in America*, ed. Mark Noll, et. al. (Grand Rapids: Wm. B. Ecrdmans Publishing Co., 1983), p. 100.

18. Ibid.

CHAPTER SIX

(pages 126-153)

1. Larry Libby, *The Cry of the Poor* (Bothell, WA: Action International Ministries, 1986), pp. 7-8.

2. Quoted in Cotton Mather, *The Great Works of Christ in America*, Vol. 2 (Edinburgh: The Banner of Truth Trust, 1979, orig. 1702), p. 148.

3. See, for example, Arthur Wallis, *God's Chosen Fast* (Fort Washington, PA: Christian Literature Crusade, 1968), pp. 94-129, 142-146; Bill Bright, *The Coming Revival* (Orlando, FL: New Life Publications, 1995), Chapters 9 and 10.

4. Rodney Clapp, "Why the Devil Takes Visa," *Christianity Today*, Oct. 7, 1996, Vol. 40, No. 2, taken from Part 3, *Christianity Online*.

5. Amy Sherman, "Hope Dreams," *Books and Culture*, May/June, 1996, pp. 3-4. She is reviewing a book by Greg Donaldson, *The Ville: Cops and Kids in Urban America* (1993) and quoting from it in part.

6. Ibid., p. 4.

7. "Why the Devil Takes Visa" (Part 3, *Christianity Online*).

8. Larry Libby, *The Cry of the Poor* (Bothell, WA: Action International Ministries, 1986), pp. 7-8.

9. Janet Ditto, "Hope on the Dump," in *Target Earth*, ed. Frank Kaleb Jansen (Kailua-Kona, HI: University of the Nations, 1989), p. 156.

10. Recounted of a real couple in *The Cry of the Poor*, pp. 11-12.

CHAPTER SEVEN

(pages 154-173)

1. William Cowper, "God Moves in a Mysterious Way," in: *Trinity Hymnal* (Philadelphia: Great Commission Publications, 1990), p. 128.

2. Michael Hamilton, "The Dissatisfaction of Francis Schaeffer," *Christianity Today*, Vol. 41, No. 3, March 3, 1997, p. 22.

3. Ibid., p. 30.

4. Francis Schaeffer, with C. Everett Koop, *Whatever Happened to the Human Race?* In: *The Complete Works of Francis Schaeffer: A Christian Worldview*, Vol. 5, *A Christian View of the West* (Wheaton, IL: Crossway Books, 1982, orig. 1979), pp. 405-406.

5. "The Dissatisfaction of Francis Schaeffer," p. 30.

6. Richard John Neuhaus, "Abortion and a Nation at War," *First Things*, No. 26, Oct. 1992, p. 12.

7. Ibid., p. 12.

8. "The Dissatisfaction of Francis Schaeffer," p. 29.

9. Francis Schaeffer, *A Christian Manifesto*, in: *The Complete Works of Francis Schaeffer: A Christian Worldview*, Vol. 5, *A Christian View of the West* (Wheaton, IL: Crossway Books, 1982, orig. 1981), p. 491.

10. "The End of Democracy: The Judicial Usurpation of Politics," *First Things*, No. 67, Nov. 1996, p. 18. The Symposium was continued in the Jan. 1997 issue, "The End of Democracy? A Discussion Continued," pp. 19-32. Remarkably this whole discussion of the Supreme Court's usurpation of politics was introduced by Francis Schaeffer fifteen years ago. He pondered out loud who might take over our government if the collapse of order came. He said, "For myself, I think we should not rule out the courts, especially the Supreme Court, as being such an elite for these reasons: 1) They are already ruling on the basis of sociological, arbitrary law. 2) They are making much law, as well as ruling on law. 3) They dominate the two other parts of government." *A Christian Manifesto*, p. 462.

11. Richard John Neuhaus, "Poor Times, Poor Country," *First Things*, No. 34, June/July 1993, p. 61.

12. "Abortion and a Nation at War," p. 13.

13. See David Reardon, *Aborted Women, Silent No More* (Chicago: Loyola University Press, 1987), with its extensive bibliography on this issue, pp. 201-202; David Reardon, *Abortion Malpractice* (Denton, TX: Life Dynamics, 1993).

14. Quoted from "Mother Teresa Speaks on Abortion," taken from the Internet Web site, www.castletown.com/teresa2.htm.

15. *A Christian Manifesto*, p. 455.

16. Ibid., p. 423.

17. Ibid., p. 494.

18. Ibid., p. 495.

19. Ibid., p. 457.

20. David Reardon, *Making Abortion Rare: A Healing Strategy for a Divided Nation* (Springfield, IL: Acorn Books, 1996), p. XV.

21. *Whatever Happened to the Human Race?*, p. 282

22. One description of the battle lines in the "Culture Wars" comes from Richard Neuhaus: "We are two nations: one concentrated on rights and laws, the other on rights and wrongs; one radically individualistic and dedicated to the actualized self, the other communal and invoking the common good; one viewing law as the instrument of the will to power and license,

the other affirming an objective moral order reflected in a Constitution to which we are obliged; one given to private satisfaction, the other to familial responsibility; one typically secular, the other typically religious; one elitist, the other populist." "Abortion and a Nation at War," p. 9.

23. *A Christian Manifesto*, p. 459.

24. Ibid., p. 457.

25. "God Moves in a Mysterious Way."

CONCLUSION

(pages 174-181)

1. Jonathan Edwards, "The Most High a Prayer-Hearing God," in *The Works of Jonathan Edwards*, Vol. 2 (Edinburgh: Banner of Truth Trust, 1974), p. 116.

2. Jonathan Edwards, *Dissertation Concerning the End for which God Created the World*, in *The Works of Jonathan Edwards*, Vol. 8, ed. Paul Ramsey (New Haven: Yale University Press, 1989), p. 526.

APPENDIX: QUOTES AND EXPERIENCES

(pages 182-210)

1. Charles Spurgeon, *Words of Counsel for Christian Workers* (Pasadena, TX: Pilgrim Publications, 1985), pp. 112-113.

NOTE ON
RESOURCES

Desiring God Ministries

The reader who wants to ponder further the vision of God and life presented in this book may be interested in the resources provided by *Desiring God Ministries* (DGM)—an extension of Bethlehem Baptist Church in Minneapolis, Minnesota. DGM exists to spread a passion for the supremacy of God in all things for the joy of all peoples by

1. producing and distributing resources for the wider Christian church that promote the vision that *God is most glorified in us when we are most satisfied in him*; and

2. appealing to non-Christians to hope in God and be satisfied with all that he is for them in Jesus.

We make all of John Piper's books available at a significant discount, and we are continually producing new audio tape, article, and manuscript collections from our archives, containing over twenty years of Dr. Piper's preaching and writing ministry. At your request we would be happy to send you a free resource catalog. We are equipped to accept VISA and MasterCard if you would like to place your order over the phone.

WHATEVER YOU CAN AFFORD!

Our goal at DGM is not to make money. Our goal is to make the treasure of the gospel as accessible to you as possible. The suggested prices in our catalog help to cover our costs, but we offer all of our resources on a *"whatever you can afford"* basis. We won't allow money to be a barrier to those who wish to receive biblical teaching for their personal use. Don't be afraid to use this policy!

FOR MORE INFORMATION:

TOLL-FREE	1-888-346-4700
ON THE WEB	www.goshen.net/dgministry/
E-MAIL	DGMinistry@aol.com
WRITE	DESIRING GOD MINISTRIES Bethlehem Baptist Church 720 Thirteenth Avenue South Minneapolis, Minnesota 55415-1793 1-612-338-7653

SCRIPTURE INDEX

PERSON
INDEX

SUBJECT
INDEX